FENG SHUI
FROM SCRATCH

FENG SHUI
FROM SCRATCH

This book is dedicated to David, Sian and Robert

JONATHAN DEE

Published by SILVERDALE BOOKS
An imprint of Bookmart Ltd
Registered number 2372865
Trading as Bookmart Ltd
Desford Road
Enderby
Leicester LE9 5AD

D&S Books
Cottage Meadow, Bocombe,
Parkham, Bideford
Devon, England
EX39 5PH

e-mail us at:-
enquiries.dspublishing@care4free.net

This edition printed 2002

ISBN 1-856056-30-9

Creative Director: Sarah King
Editor: Liz Dean
Project editor: Judith Millidge
Photographer: Paul Forrester
Designer: Axis Design

Printed in Singapore

1 3 5 7 9 10 8 6 4 2

Contents

Introduction

Feng Shui has been practised in China for many centuries. It exists to bring man and his creations into tune with the natural forces which surround him. The name Feng Shui literally translates as 'wind and water', because as the name implies the energies, or chi, of heaven and earth should be allowed to flow gently through our lives, like a gentle stream or a pleasant breeze.

Although the antiquity of Feng Shui places it amongst the oldest forms of continuous knowledge, it is more in tune with modern thinking now than it has been for centuries. After all, it can be thought of as the original environmental philosophy.

Despite its legendary beginnings, Feng Shui is not some half-remembered tradition left over from the days when an emperor sat

on the Dragon Throne in the Forbidden City.
The ancient Taoist masters whose wisdom gave
rise to Feng Shui thought that its correct use would
create a perfect environment, and that it would also
promote health, happiness and prosperity for
those who lived in such harmonious
surroundings.

It is an art form that is very much alive
and has now spread worldwide,
bringing practical and spiritual
benefits to all who
subscribe to its
teachings.

The Cosmic Principles

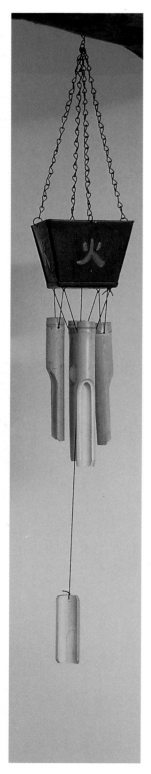

To get to grips with Feng Shui, you first need to grasp some of the basic principles involved. However, this is not something to be worried about because, they are explained here very simply. They include chi, which is the universal breath of life; the opposing concepts of yang and yin; the five elements of Wood, Fire, Earth, Metal and Water; the Feng Shui map, known as the Lo Shu Magic Square; your personal Star Number and the significance of the eight directions of the compass.

What is Chi?

The ancient philosophers who created the concepts of oriental mysticism were convinced that the universe was filled with an animating force. This essential life-force was called chi.

Chi has no direct parallel in western culture.

The gentle movements and harmonious tones of a windchime enhance the flow of chi. It is particularly useful in an area where the chi is stagnant.

Harmonious energy or sheng chi is said to move like a gentle breeze or a bubbling stream. This gives rise to the very name Feng Shui, which literally means 'wind and water'.

Spiritually, it can be thought of as divine inspiration from angels or gods or, for the purposes of Feng Shui, as the very fuel on which the cosmos runs. And like the best eco-friendly system, chi creates positive energy as a by-product of its existence.

Chi flows around us and through us. It is created by light, movement and life and, at its best, it energizes and enriches both our world and us. This positive, free-flowing chi, correctly known as sheng chi, is a life-enhancer, creating both luck and health as it moves; its presence in the art of Feng Shui is definitely encouraged. Luck-bearing sheng chi is thought to move in sinuous, meandering paths, flowing in exactly the same way as gentle breezes and streams. In fact this association of luck with wind and water gives rise to the literal translation of Feng Shui (feng meaning 'wind' and shui, 'water'). Positive chi likes

Above: Clutter can create misfortune-bearing chi, called sha chi.

Right: A long, empty corridor allows even positive chi to become a secret arrow moving too quickly to distribute good fortune.

curves to aid its passage, but straight lines, such as empty hallways or corridors with doors at each end, speed up chi, so that it zooms past, never pausing to distribute its bounty of fortunate influences.

If, however, the free passage of sheng chi is blocked or disrupted in some way, then the energy becomes stagnant. Like still water, the energy-pool will fester, transforming previously good influences into bad ones. This stagnant, misfortune-bearing chi is called sha chi. It is present in dusty, neglected corners, and in and around clutter-mountains and general garbage. An environment drowning in sha chi is often recognized as suffering from Sick Building Syndrome, and its occupants are likely to be prone to ill-health, depression and bad luck. Obviously, good Feng Shui is about minimizing such situations by both prevention and cure, and at all times striving to create a balanced environment.

Yang and Yin

The concept of yang and yin derives from the ancient Chinese religious philosophy known as Taoism. The word Tao literally means 'the way', expressing the way, or harmony, of the natural world. Taoism holds that if we live in a sympathetic manner with nature, then only good can result, both in this life and in our future existence.

Sheng chi (the fortunate kind of chi) is thought to be in constant motion between yang and yin. The more that sheng chi moves, the greater its force. Therefore, maintaining a balance between yang and yin in your environment encourages positive energy, and is vital to good Feng Shui.

Yang is the positive, active component of chi. Its nature is bright, upwardly moving, masculine and lively. Its opposite, yin, is dark and heavy, tending to move downwards, and is feminine, receptive and passive. Remember that when we are dealing with ancient oriental descriptions that they do tend to be very traditional – for example, it should never be thought that yang is considered good and yin bad. On the contrary, one could not exist without the other, and indeed they can only exist in reference to each other. That which is not yang therefore must be yin, and vice versa.

Yang and yin can be likened to the opposite poles of a magnet. Yin would represent the principle of attraction, because it is passive, while yang would tend to repel because it is active. Similarly, we can think of these cosmic opposites as night and day, hot and cold, summer and winter, big and small, and so on. Below is a list of complementary opposites associated with yang and yin. Of course, this list is not by any means exhaustive.

The philosophers who devised this system of classification suggested that yang and yin also contain the 'seed' of their opposite, linking them inextricably. This gave rise to the popular Tai chi, or yin-yang, symbol, in which there is a small circle of darkness within the light area, and a circle of light within the darkness.

At its heart, Feng Shui is concerned with maintaining a perfect balance between yang and yin, so that beneficial sheng chi can flow through our environments and lives. When we are contented and happy in our surroundings, yang and yin are in harmony both inside and outside of ourselves.

The complementary concepts of yang and yin are usually depicted as the circular Tai Chi symbol. In this famous illustration, there is a seed of light in the darkness and vice versa showing the inextricable links of yang and yin.

yang	yin
Male	Female
Light	Dark
Hot	Cold
Light	Heavy
Hard	Soft
Positive	Negative
Heaven	Earth
Fire	Water
Mountain	Valley
Sharp	Blunt
Sour	Sweet
Right	Left
Up	Down
Front	Back
Spirit	Body
Solid	Hollow
Angular	Curved
Odd	Even
Moving	Static
Day	Night
Sun	Moon

The height of mountains reaching towards heaven and the rough, unyielding rocky outcrops emphasize the powerfully masculine nature of yang energy

The depth of water and the fact that water is both acted upon and will assume the shape of its container tends to make it yin in nature.

The Five Elements

In western mystic traditions, which partly derive from the philosophies of ancient Greece, there are said to be four elements. These are Earth, Water, Air and Fire, expressing the four states of matter: solid, liquid, gaseous and pure energy. Before our modern, technological age everything was thought to be made of combinations of these four basic ingredients. However, in China, the birthplace of Feng Shui, Taoist philosophers preferred a five-fold classification. Unlike their western counterparts, they did not believe that things were literally made up of these elements, but were of the opinion that they represented a sort of evolution, a sequence of changes from one state of being to another. This is why the five Chinese elements are more correctly called 'Agents of Change', or simply 'The Transformations'.

The five elements of Taoist tradition are Wood (Mu), Fire (Huo), Earth (T'u), Metal (Chin) and Water (Shui, as in Feng Shui). Each of these elements represents a principle of existence, and when acting together in this order they become what is known as the Cycle of Creation. This is because Wood provides fuel for Fire; Fire creates Earth in the form of ash; deep in the earth, Metal is formed, and the condensation on metal surfaces creates Water. Water, of course, provides nourishment for Wood.

This is the most harmonious arrangement of the element cycle. However, if the elements were to skip the next in line and were immediately followed by the next but one, then this results in the Cycle of Destruction. Wood drains and exhausts Earth; Earth pollutes Water, making it muddy; Water douses Fire; Fire melts Metal, and finally, Metal chops Wood.

The Cycle of Creation

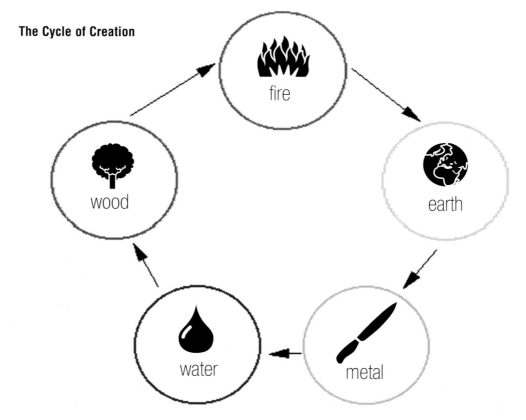

Wood fuels Fire.
Fire creates Earth.
Earth creates Metal.
Metal creates Water.
Water feeds Wood.

The Cycle of Destruction

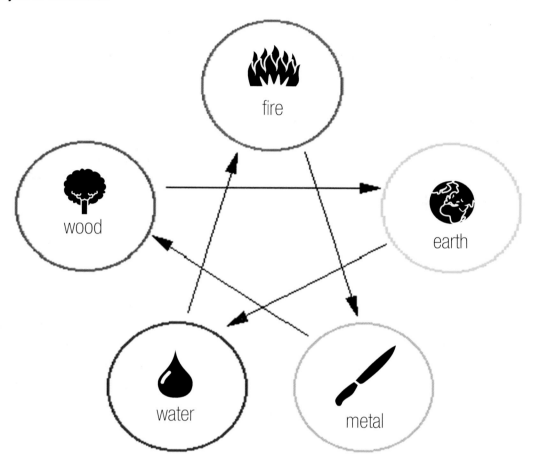

Wood exhausts Earth.

Earth pollutes Water.

Water douses Fire.

Fire melts Metal.

Metal chops Wood.

There is also a neutral cycle which, in effect, is the Cycle of Creation backwards in the order of Water, Metal, Earth, Fire and Wood. However, as its name implies, this has little or no effect upon your environment.

Elemental Conflict

The five elements are extremely helpful when they are in the productive Cycle of Creation. However, they can be very harmful when they are placed together in the Cycle of Destruction. For example, the destructive cycle is the reason that it is not a good idea to have a bathroom at the centre of your dwelling. The bathroom (see page 107–111) is by nature ruled by the Water element, and the centre of the house by the Earth element. If you refer to the Cycle of Destruction you will see that Earth pollutes Water. Likewise, the kitchen (see pages 83–87) which is governed by both Fire and Water can be an elemental danger area. Both these cases constitute elemental conflict. The solution to this problem is to effectively transform the destructive cycle into its more auspicious counterpart by the addition of another element. In the case of the bathroom with a Water-Earth conflict, the addition of Metal would restore a healthy balance. In the kitchen, a conflict between Fire and Water can be resolved by the addition of Wood.

Of course, one need not literally add Fire when that element is the resolution to a conflict. Something red, triangular or suggestive of flame or

In kitchens there is often a conflict between fire and water as the oven and sink are opposite each other. Here, the two elements exist side by side..

the South would do just as well. Equally, if you were having trouble in a Metal-ruled area of your home, possibly because you had a hearth or oven there (the Fire element), one Feng Shui remedy would be to add a yellow rug, an attractive stone or bring in a yellow theme to your décor. This is because these are all symbols of the element of Earth, which is the solution to a Metal-Fire conflict. The same technique applies to any other elemental problem, both in the home and in the garden. Remember, these are merely suggestions — it is up to you to use the governing principles of Feng Shui in a tasteful and imaginative manner. Mastering this aspect of Feng Shui is easy with a little elementary thinking.

The Elemental Directions

The cycles of creation and destruction are a vital ingredient of the art of Feng Shui, because each of

the elements is associated with one of the eight directions of the compass plus the centre, which is ruled by the Earth element. Therefore, each area of your home and garden is associated with an element. The physical features, contents and function of any given area can either be in harmony or in conflict with the elemental rulership. Unfortunate compass locations for rooms as well as wall and fabric colours that antagonize a room's element are thought to be responsible for disharmony. Check the elements and their associated directions opposite – you will need to refer back to this when working out the ruling elements for the rooms in your home.

The cardinal directions of East, South, West and North are the most important and are symbolized by the Green Dragon of the East, the Red Bird of the South, the White Tiger of the West and the Black

Tortoise of the North. These animals symbolize the type of energy that arrives at your home and garden, and they are treated separately under 'Chi and the Symbolic Animals', page 30–35.

Designing with the Elements

As well as being directional, the elements have many symbolic associations which are helpful when deciding what should go into any given area to make it elementally compatible. Below is a list of suggested shapes, colours and images.

Element Design Guide

The most important elemental direction is called the facing direction. This is the direction in which your front door (or mainly-used entrance) faces. For instance, if your front door faces West, then the prevailing element of your house will be Metal, and your fate in that abode will be determined by the fierce energies of the White Tiger (see page 35). If the door faces South, then the governing element will be Fire and the creative energies of the Red Bird or Phoenix come into play (see page 34). The rest of the elements will then be distributed about your property in accordance with a diagram called the Lo Shu Magic Square (see page 16).

Personalizing Your Feng Shui

Now you can add another factor to elemental Feng Shui. You, too, have a governing element, which is based on your date of birth. This personal element may, or may not, be in tune with the elemental bias of your home. To discover this, you need to work out your personal Star Number (see pages 22–23) according to the Lo Shu Magic Square.

It would be good Feng Shui to place items which are suggestive of the sea such as shells in the northern sector of the home because this is the area which is governed by the element Water.

	Element	Direction	Colours	Image	Shape
🌳	WOOD	East, south-east	Green, light blue	Dragon	▭
🔥	FIRE	South	Red, purple	Phoenix	△
🌍	EARTH	Centre, North-west, South-east	Yellow	Emperor	☐
🔪	METAL	West, North-west	White, metallic	Tiger	○
💧	WATER	North	Black, Dark blue	Tortoise	≈

What is the Lo Shu Magic Square?

This is one of the most ancient aspects of Chinese philosophy. The Lo Shu Magic Square is used in Feng Shui and also in a branch of Chinese astrology known as Nine Star Chi. In the Orient, this is as familiar as the twelve signs of the zodiac in the West.

The Lo Shu is said to have been discovered on the back of a riverbank turtle by the semi-mythical Emperor Yu during some improbably remote era (estimated to be 2200 BC). Hence the grid is called the Lo Shu, or 'River Diagram'.

The Magic Square is basically a 3 x 3 grid of small squares, each of which is allocated a number (the very ones supposedly discovered on the turtle's back). There are eight possible ways to add up the numbers, the sum of which will always be fifteen. Each of the small squares has a specific meaning and associations.

the Lo Shu magic square

	SE	S	SW
SE	4	9	2	SW
E	3	5	7	W
NE	8	1	6	NW

The Meanings of the Squares

1 The Career Square

This is the area of your home that relates to your career and purpose in life. It can also show an aspect of your self-image, as well as the role that you play in society. Business dealings can also be represented here, so this area is particularly important to the ambitious.

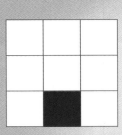

2 The Relationship Square

This is the area that represents personal relationships. Romance, especially, is dealt with here, including marriage and other long-standing partnerships. It is a particularly important area for those whose emotional life is rocky or troublesome.

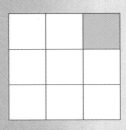

3 The Ancestors Square

This is traditionally regarded as one of the most important of the Lo Shu squares. It deals with the past, with ancestors and their spirits. Keeping the ancestors happy was a preoccupation for the Chinese, who believed that the spirits governed the fortunes of the living. Family relationships with your elders and your prospects of gaining an inheritance are also governed by this area.

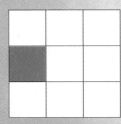

4 The Wealth Square

The financial fortunes and the prospect of wealth are found in area 4. The possibilities of gaining and retaining money can be considerably improved by the good maintenance of this area.

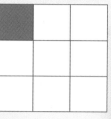

The things one truly values can be represented here, too, both material and sentimental, so it is a good idea to keep something you treasure in this part of your home.

5 The Health Square

Health issues and physical wellbeing are shown in this square. The prospects of recovery from illness will be improved by keeping this area clean, tidy and tasteful-

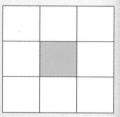

ly decorated. The balance of yang and yin is particularly important in this sector, as indeed is the harmony of the elements.

6 The Divinity Square

In oriental tradition this is the sector sacred to the gods. If you are religiously inclined, this is a good place for meaningful imagery. It is also said that a written prayer left here

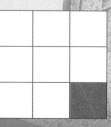

has more chance of being answered. Be that as it may, the area also represents helpful influences and people who are well disposed towards you. It is a good area in which to display mementoes of friendship.

7 The Creative Square

This is the sector of children, fertility and creation. Its energies may also manifest as your hobbies or as creative gifts. If you want to be more expressive with your talents,

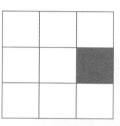

then the energies of this area should be encouraged by careful Feng Shui. This applies even if you want more enjoyable leisure time.

8 The Education Square

This sector relates to education and the use of knowledge. It can also show how open you are to new ideas. More broadly, it also refers to novelty coming into your life

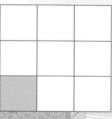

and how you are likely to react to it. It is an area to be encouraged if you feel that you are in something of a rut and need a boost to add some excitement to your existence.

9 The Fame Square

This is the area of fame governing your reputation in the world at large. Subtle interpretation of this area can reveal how you are viewed by others and the extent of their

respect for you. If you feel overlooked or humiliated in some way, then special attention paid to this area will improve your status.

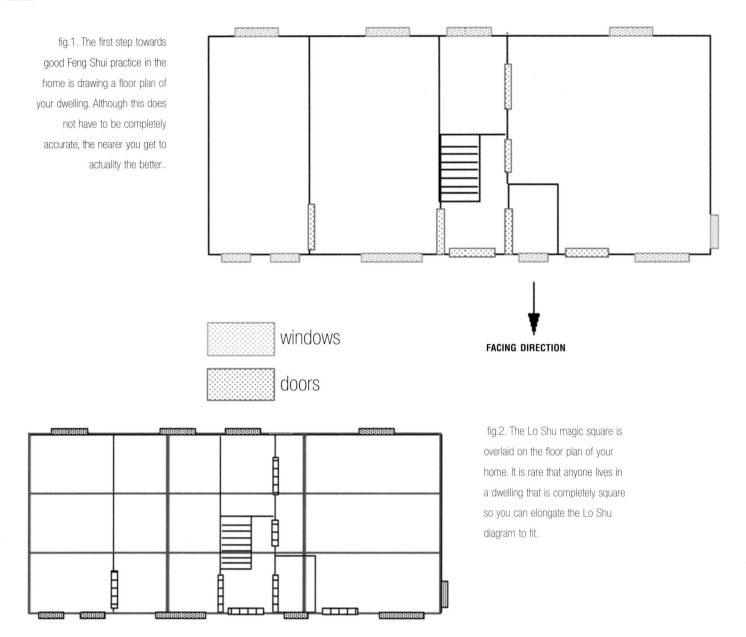

fig.1. The first step towards good Feng Shui practice in the home is drawing a floor plan of your dwelling. Although this does not have to be completely accurate, the nearer you get to actuality the better..

windows

doors

FACING DIRECTION

fig.2. The Lo Shu magic square is overlaid on the floor plan of your home. It is rare that anyone lives in a dwelling that is completely square so you can elongate the Lo Shu diagram to fit.

The Lo Shu is used in many ways in Chinese culture, but in this book we will deal with it only as it applies to space. In Feng Shui planning, the grid is overlaid on a floor plan of your home to tell you which sectors of your house and garden relate to specific areas of your life. To accomplish this, draw a rough floor plan of your house or apartment (fig. 1). It is likely that your plan won't be exactly square, but this is not a problem because you simply elongate the Lo Shu to fit the available space (fig. 2), taking special note of any sector that falls outside your home. Now square off your plan by filling in any missing sectors with a dotted line. Then, find the true centre of your home by simply drawing diagonal lines from corner to corner of your squared-off plan (fig. 3). It is also a good idea to use different-coloured pens to represent actu-

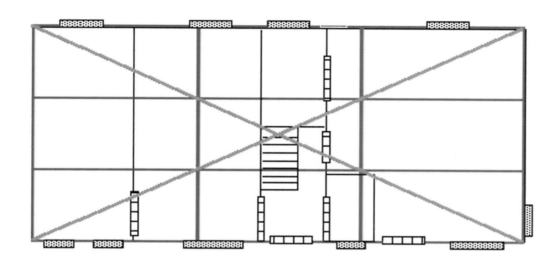

fig.3. To find the exact centre of your home, draw two diagonal lines from corner to corner. Where they intersect will be the exact central point which is governed by the Earth element.

The mainly used doorway of your home (usually the front door) will be located in areas 8, 1 or 6 in the Lo Shu Magic Square.

al features such as walls, doors and windows, and to fill in the spiritual aspects associated with areas of the superimposed Lo Shu.

The front door (or main entrance) will be located in squares 8, 1 or 6, depending on the map of your home. It follows that square 5 will occupy the centre of your home and squares 4, 9 and 2, the rear.

The Eight-Point Method

If you don't have time to map out your abode precisely (although I strongly recommend that you do) you can use the easier Eight-point Method. It is very simple indeed because when you stand at the centre of any given space, in this case your home, you will be surrounded by the eight significant areas. To do this, simply face the same direction as the front of your dwelling and the Lo Shu will fall into place about you. You are standing in the area of health (square 5). To your left is square 7, the area of creativity and children. To your right is Square 3, the area of ancestors. Directly in front is the career area, square 1, while fame and reputation is directly behind you (Square 9). The other squares will neatly fill in the gaps. Make a note of these areas, and see pages 16–17 for the associations of the squares with different areas of your life.

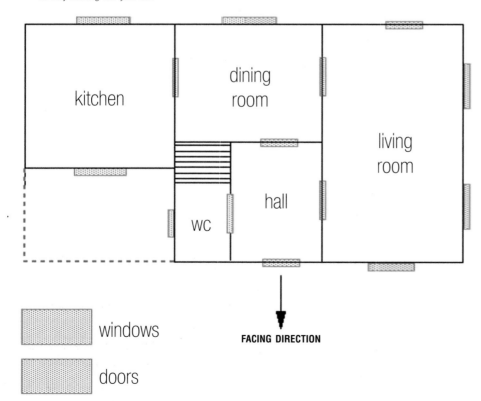

fig.4. An irregular dwelling such as a house which is L shaped should be 'squared off' to provide a suitable template for the Lo Shu square. Such a dwelling will inevitably mean that one or more significant areas will be missing..

fig.5. In this case, the missing area corresponds to sector 8 in the Lo Shu square relating to education and the use of knowledge. This sector also governs the readiness to accept novelty coming into your life.

FACING DIRECTION

windows

doors

Missing and Enlarged Areas

If the Lo Shu does not fit neatly within your four walls because you home is irregularly shaped, then there is likely to be a 'void' area in your life. For example, an L-shaped dwelling could easily have one or two sectors missing,which could damage fortunes in the areas that these sectors represent.

If a Lo Shu sector is missing in your home, you can hang a mirror or two on the walls that boundary the 'missing' sectors. This provides an illusion of space. The best place for these mirrors is where the corner-to-corner diagonal lines on your plan meet the outside wall of the dwelling.

Enlarged areas of a dwelling can also cause problems. Many dwellings have extensions that could unbalance the Feng Shui of the home. This often means that the occupants are spending too much time and attention on one aspect of their lives at the expense of others.

An exaggerated sector can be dealt with by checking the direction and associated element of that area, and using one of the cures for elemental conflicts on page 13.

windows

doors

It is rare for anyone to live in a home that is perfectly square or rectangular. Indeed many flats and apartments have an extremely irregular shape, effectively cutting out many sectors of the Lo Shu. If your home is so peculiar in shape that it is impossible to overlay the Lo Shu successfully then there is another option: apply the Lo Shu to each of the rooms individually, so you have a mini-Lo Shu for each area.

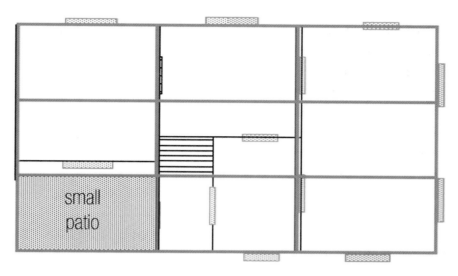

small patio

If at all possible, missing areas should be integrated into home design. In this case the addition of a small patio to fill the blank space will give scope for a pleasing design, plant life or a water feature to enliven the space.

The rule about filling voids applies to the interior of the home as well. The addition of a pleasing mirror on an otherwise blank wall can have beneficial effects in Feng Shui terms.

Star Numbers and Feng Shui

This form of oriental divination is very simple indeed, yet its impact on one's life and future can be profound. Working out your personal Star Number will reveal your lucky and unlucky directions and a suitable choice of symbols and colour co-ordinates that are most auspicious for your home and garden.

The Star Numbers form a branch of Chinese astrology related to the Lo Shu, and like the more familiar animal signs of the oriental zodiac, are dependent on your year of birth.

Just as with the animal signs, the changeover of Star Numbers begins at Chinese New Year. Officially the date for this event is February 4th, but it can be between January 20th and February 18th. So if you were born in January, it is likely that you were born under the Star Number and the animal sign for the previous year. For example, January 13th 1992 will actually be calculated as belonging to the previous year of 1991. Remember that in this form of astrology, only the year of birth is important.

Star Number Associations

Star Number	Ruling Element	Fortunate Directions
1	Water	N, SE, W, N
2	Earth	SW, NE, W, S
3	Wood	E, S, SE, N
4	Wood	SE, N, S, E
5 (male)	Earth	NE, SW, W, NW
5 (female)	Earth	SW, NE, W, S
6	Metal	NW, W, SW, N, NE
7	Metal	W, NW, SW, N, NE
8	Earth	NE, SW, W, NW
9	Fire	S, E, SE, SW, NE

The next step is to take the last two digits of your year of birth and add them together. For example, in the case of 1991, take the last two numbers and add them: 9 + 1 = 10. If, as in this case, you arrive at a sum that is more than nine, add the new numbers like so: 1 + 0 = 1.

If you are female, now add 5: 1 + 5 = 6. However, if you are male you must subtract your original answer from 10: 10 - 1 = 9. So, from the same year calculation there is a considerable difference in the answer for men and women; this divergence is due to yang and yin principles (see page 10). This is also the reason why number 5 is counted twice, with separate lucky directions for men and women. 5 is considered to be the most changeable of the numbers and, therefore, more prone to the vagaries of yang and yin.

Three Steps to Calculating Your Star Number

Step 1 Take the last two digits of your year of birth (remember that if you were born before Chinese New Year, count it as the previous year) and add them together.

Step 2 If you arrive at a number higher than 9 then add these two new digits together again until you arrive at a number between 1 and 9.

Step 3 For women, add 5 to your answer. Again, if you arrive at a number greater than 9, add the two digits together until you arrive at an answer which is between 1 and 9. This will be your personal Star Number. For men, subtract your answer from 10.

See the Star Number tables opposite to check that you have worked out your Star Number correctly. Of course, this is a very simplified approach to Chinese astrology, but for the purposes of Feng Shui this basic calculation is enough to reveal your ruling element and thus your affinity or otherwise with certain compass directions.

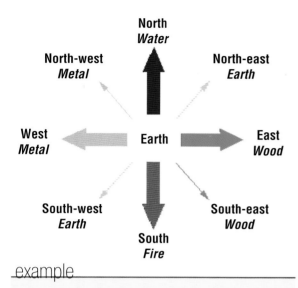

North
Water

North-west
Metal

North-east
Earth

West
Metal

Earth

East
Wood

South-west
Earth

South-east
Wood

South
Fire

example

David was born in 1961. Since he was not born before Chinese New Year, we take the last two digits of his birth year and add them together: 6 + 1 = 7. (If he had been born in early January we would have taken the last two digits of the previous year.) We now follow the Star Number rule for men and subtract 7 from 10, arriving at a Star Number of 3. According to this system, the number 3 is ruled by the Wood element, associated with the East, the South-east, the South and also the North. Any of these directions will bring David luck. They also point out areas of his home and garden that are advantageous to him and, by omission, the directions that may be troublesome and therefore need Feng Shui expertise to bring them into harmony.

Sarah was born in 1967 after Chinese New Year, so we add the last two digits of the birth year: 6 + 7 = 13. Since this is a number higher than 9, we add these two digits 1 + 3 = 4. We now follow the Star Number rule for women and add 5: 4 + 5 = 9. So Sarah's personal Star Number is 9. This number is ruled by the Fire element and is aligned primarily to the South, but with affiliations with the East, South-east, North-east and also with the South-west.

The relationship between David and Sarah is therefore a positive and enriching one, because their elemental bias as revealed by their respective Star Numbers places them in the Cycle of Creation (see page 12). Wood fuels Fire, therefore it is reasonable to deduce that Sarah is emotionally supported by David because his ruling element precedes hers. It is also possible to deduce that both are creative and talented people, although Sarah is more likely to be artistically gifted because of her connection to the inspiring influence of the Fire element. The pair also share many of their fortunate directions having East, South-east and the South in common as auspicious areas of luck, health and prosperity.

year numbers for men

9	8	7	6	5	4	3	2	1
1901	1902	1903	1904	1905	1906	1907	1908	1909
1910	1911	1912	1913	1914	1915	1916	1917	1918
1919	1920	1921	1922	1923	1924	1925	1926	1927
1928	1929	1930	1931	1932	1933	1934	1935	1936
1937	1938	1939	1940	1941	1942	1943	1944	1945
1946	1947	1948	1949	1950	1951	1952	1953	1954
1955	1956	1957	1958	1959	1960	1961	1962	1963
1964	1965	1966	1967	1968	1969	1970	1971	1972
1973	1974	1975	1976	1977	1978	1979	1980	1981
1982	1983	1984	1985	1986	1987	1988	1989	1990
1991	1992	1993	1994	1995	1996	1997	1998	1999
2000	2001	2002	2003	2004	2005	2006	2007	2008
2009	2010	2011	2012	2013	2014	2015	2016	2017

year numbers for women

6	7	8	9	1	2	3	4	5
1901	1902	1903	1904	1905	1906	1907	1908	1909
1910	1911	1912	1913	1914	1915	1916	1917	1918
1919	1920	1921	1922	1923	1924	1925	1926	1927
1928	1929	1930	1931	1932	1933	1934	1935	1936
1937	1938	1939	1940	1941	1942	1943	1944	1945
1946	1947	1948	1949	1950	1951	1952	1953	1954
1955	1956	1957	1958	1959	1960	1961	1962	1963
1964	1965	1966	1967	1968	1969	1970	1971	1972
1973	1974	1975	1976	1977	1978	1979	1980	1981
1982	1983	1984	1985	1986	1987	1988	1989	1990
1991	1992	1993	1994	1995	1996	1997	1998	1999
2000	2001	2002	2003	2004	2005	2006	2007	2008
2009	2010	2011	2012	2013	2014	2015	2016	2017

What your star number means

Star number 1

Element: Water
Primary Fortunate Direction: North
Colours: Black (for Water) but also white, silver or transparent
Associated trigram: K'an, 'The Abysmal'

Symbol: Water
Bodily associations: Kidneys, bladder, sexual organs, bones, nervous system
Symbolic animals: Pig, rat, fox, bat

Advantageous occupations: Social worker, printing and dyeing, fishing industry, chemist, philosopher, dairy worker, restaurateur, writer, bartender, lawyer, maintenance operative, masseur
Compatible with Star Numbers: 6, 7, 3, 4
Incompatible with: 1, 2, 8, 9

Basic characteristics: 1 Water people are far too individualistic to be team players. They are deep thinkers who may brood over imagined insults. They are rarely attracted to leadership positions, even though they do not lack self-motivation or discipline.

Health advice: Being prone to kidney and bladder complaints, 1 Water people should avoid too much salt and sugar and wrap up warm in cold weather.

Star number 2

Element: Earth
Primary fortunate direction: South-west
Colours: Yellow (for Earth) but also black or dark blue
Associated trigram: Kun, 'The Receptive'

Symbol: Earth
Bodily associations: Abdomen, stomach, spleen
Symbolic Animals: Cow, mare, ant

Advantageous occupations: Mother, carer, union member, doctor, nurse, antique dealer, gardener, grocer, civil engineer, farmer
Compatible with Star Numbers: 9, 6, 7
Incompatible with: 1, 2, 3, 4

Basic characteristics: 2 Earth people are carers who look after people around them. They are great organisers who love to entertain. They feel the need to be part of a team, and are very co-operative. However, they can be overly fussy and prone to needless worry.

Health advice: A sensible diet without too much sugar, coffee or alcohol is recommended. Aromatherapy and gentle massage can relieve stress.

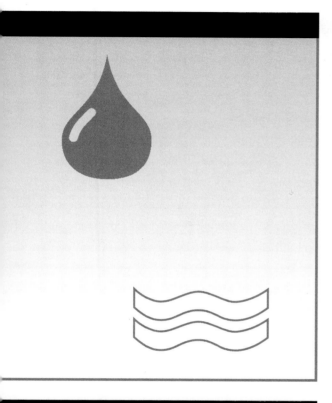

Star number 3

Element: Wood

Primary fortunate direction: East

Colours: Bright green and indigo

Associated trigram: Chen, 'The Arousing'

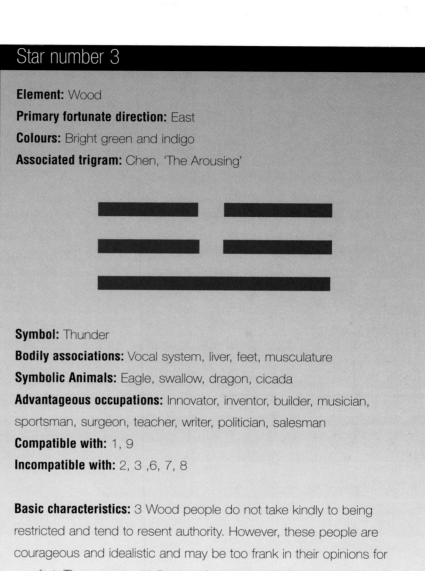

Symbol: Thunder

Bodily associations: Vocal system, liver, feet, musculature

Symbolic Animals: Eagle, swallow, dragon, cicada

Advantageous occupations: Innovator, inventor, builder, musician, sportsman, surgeon, teacher, writer, politician, salesman

Compatible with: 1, 9

Incompatible with: 2, 3 ,6, 7, 8

Basic characteristics: 3 Wood people do not take kindly to being restricted and tend to resent authority. However, these people are courageous and idealistic and may be too frank in their opinions for comfort. They are great talkers and can worm their way out of most problems.

Health advice: Fatty foods and alcohol can cause problems to the liver and gall bladder. Also, the muscles, tendons and ligaments need extra care.

Star number 4

Element: Wood

Primary fortunate direction: South-east

Colours: Rich dark-green

Associated trigram: Sun, 'The Gentle'

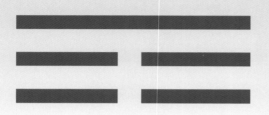

Symbol: Wind

Bodily associations:

Lungs, gall bladder and legs (4 Wood people often possess rather hypnotic eyes)

Symbolic animals: Cock, chicken, crane, snake, unicorn and earthworm

Advantageous occupations: Shipping, building, furnishing, advertising, travel, mediator, communications, teaching, public relations, also the manufacture or selling of wood or rope

Compatible with Star Numbers: 1, 9

Incompatible with: 2 ,4, 6, 7, 8

Basic characteristics: 4 Wood people appear to be cool and calm. However, inside, they are tense and rather vulnerable, becoming moody and stubborn when under pressure. They have great common sense and are innovative thinkers.

Health advice: Just like the 3 Wood type, alcohol and fatty foods can cause problems. Gentle exercise to tone up the muscles, ligaments and tendons is recommended.

Star number 5

Element: Earth

Primary fortunate directions: South-west and North-east

Colour: Yellow

Associated trigrams: Kun, 'The Receptive', and Ken, 'Keeping Still'

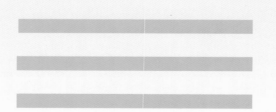

Symbols: Earth and mountain, respectively

Bodily associations: Hands, abdomen, stomach, pancreas, spleen and lymphatic system

Symbolic animals: None

Advantageous occupations: Politician, captain of industry, military or police officer, second-hand dealer, labourer

Compatible with Star Numbers: 9, 6, 7

Incompatible with: 1, 3, 4

Basic characteristics: 5 Earth people tend to be eccentric. They love to be at the centre of things and influence those around them in a positive way. Decent, honest and loyal, they can nevertheless make enemies who dislike their candour.

Health advice: Anything to reduce blood pressure is a good idea for 5 Earth types. Positive thinking, too, will help periodic bouts of anxiety.

Star number 6

Element: Metal

Primary fortunate direction: North-west

Colour: White, gold

Associated trigram: Ch'ien, 'The Creative'

Symbol: Heaven

Bodily associations: Skull, head, pineal gland, lungs, large intestine, skin

Symbolic animals: Tiger, lion, horse

Advantageous occupations: Leader, government service, industrialist, jeweller, salesman, sportsman, priest, teacher, psychiatrist, counsellor, manager, lawyer

Compatible with Star Numbers: 2, 5, 8, 1

Incompatible with: 3, 4, 6, 9

Basic characteristics: 6 Metal people have strong personalities, are loyal and make superb advisors. They are orderly, responsible and often highly moral. Very hard-working, they may find that close relationships suffer because they simply do not have enough time for them.

Health advice: Congestion, skin problems and periodic headaches are associated with this number, all of which are due to tension, so making time for relaxation is important.

Star number 7

Element: Metal

Primary fortunate direction: West

Colours: White (for metal) and red

Associated trigram: Tui, 'The Joyous'

Symbol: Lake

Bodily associations: Lips, the mouth, speech organs, lungs, large intestine, skin

Symbolic animals: Sheep, birds, deer, elk and ape

Advantageous occupations: Public relations, entertainment industries, banking and financial management, lecturer, dentist, spokesperson, publican

Compatible with Star Numbers: 1, 2, 5, 8

Incompatible with: 3, 4, 7, 9

Basic Characteristics: Attractive, amusing and intelligent, 7 Metal people enjoy the good life, and are outgoing and cheerful with a tremendous sense of style. However, they may also be self-indulgent, and go a long way to avoid confrontations.

Health advice: The chest is a weak spot as indeed are the bowels. Attention to diet is important to avoid stomach irritations, and do try to avoid smoking.

Star number 8

Element: Earth

Primary fortunate direction: North-east

Colours: Yellow (for Earth) and white

Associated trigram: Ken, 'Keeping Still'

Symbol: Mountain

Bodily associations: Hands, back, spleen, pancreas, stomach

Symbolic animals: Dog, bull, ox, leopard and mouse

Advantageous occupations: Clerical, the clergy, sculpting, civil service, beautician

Compatible with Star Numbers: 6, 7, 9

Incompatible with: 1, 3, 4

Basic characteristics: 8 Earth people are hard workers who are meticulous about detail. They tend to be slow, thorough, single-minded and capable of great determination. They have a clam exterior and make great counsellors. However, sometimes they are very indecisive.

Health advice: Positive mental attitudes will combat despondency, and care with the diet will avoid constipation. Aches and pains in the joints can be another concern.

Star number 9

Element: Fire

Primary fortunate direction: South

Colours: Dark wine-red (for Fire), purple, orange

Associated trigram: Li, 'The Clinging'

Symbol: Fire

Bodily associations: Blood, heart, small intestine, glands

Symbolic animals: Pheasant, phoenix, goldfish, crab, shrimp, oyster, turtle, partridge, sparrow

Advantageous occupations: Writer, artist, craftsman, book dealer, beautician, diplomat, lawyer, fortune-teller, advertising agent, broker, garden designer

Compatible with Star Numbers: 2, 3, 4, 5, 8

Incompatible with: 1, 6, 7, 9

Basic characteristics: 9 Fire people are charismatic and enjoy the limelight. They have a strong sense of rightness and are probably artistically gifted in some way. Their main faults are that they may trust others too much, and they can be quite vain.

Health advice: Blood pressure can be affected by tension.
Regular eye tests will spot potential problems before they occur.

As you become more familiar with the Lo Shu Magic Square, you will notice that the numbers of compatibility and incompatibility refer both to people born within the associated years, and also with fortunate and unfortunate points of the compass. The colours associated with the individual directions can also be incorporated into the décor of the appropriate areas of your home and garden to help bring these into greater harmony.

Chi and the Symbolic Animals

Before we study the eight directions of the compass and their associated trigrams, we must examine the all-important cardinal directions of North, South, East and West which constitute what is known as the Four Palaces of the Symbolic Animals.

Each animal is symbolic of the type of energy, or chi, that flows towards your home and garden. The facing direction plays a vital role in this (see Garden Entry page 112 and the Front Door, page 50). The animal that governs the facing direction will set the tone for the entire home, as well as determining the nature of the fortunes of the occupants.

It is also important to bear in mind that the chi entering your personal space can be compromised by features in your immediate locality. A nearby cemetery, refuse dump or dirty industrial estate will add negative sha chi to your home environment. However, a cemetery in the North, or Palace of the Black Tortoise, is thought of as the right and proper direction for death to manifest itself.

In Feng Shui the East and the West, the Palaces of the Green Dragon and White Tiger, are the most important. The creative Dragon symbolizes the yang of the rising sun and of springtime. The yin of the White Tiger, on the other hand, embodies dusk and the autumn or Fall.

It is thought that the perfect site for a home is at the place where the Green Dragon and the White

The eastern view from the main door of the house has a quite extraordinary representation of the Green Dragon detectable in the shape of the trees which crest the hill.

Tiger mate. Or, to put it less poetically, where the characteristics of the surrounding landscape allow the maximum amount of chi to accumulate. This means that to maximize the fortunes of a household, the East should in some way physically resemble the Dragon's back. Hills, rooftops or lofty trees in this direction are fortuitous. The White Tiger's profile immediately to the West should be ideally be lower than that of the Dragon, and present a more rounded view. This is why it is recommended that a detached house should have a low wall to the West to symbolize the Tiger; likewise, a high wall to the East would provide the profile of the Dragon, if no suitable physical feature already exists. Of course in ancient China, the physical landscape was considered so important that if no feature representing the animal existed, then the command of the Emperor would be to build one!

Furthering this idea, the North, the Palace of the Black Tortoise, should support a building like the

Traditionally, the land to the West should be lower than that of the east. Here it is symbolised by a valley and a lower hill on the western side. Remarkably, the striped pattern made by farm machinery does indeed suggest the stripes of the White Tiger.

Above: The rounded, tree covered hill to the North is a good representation of the shell of the Black Tortoise, the symbolic animal of that direction.

Right: It's a good idea to look at the natural features surrounding your home to spot the symbolic animals 'hiding' in the landscape. Although this may not be so easy in the city, rooftops, walls and other features will conceal the four directional beasts.

back of a chair and, like a horseshoe, protect its occupants from the evils of that direction. This is the reason that the Great Wall of China serves more than a defensive purpose. It also symbolizes support in the North for the whole of the country.

A Feng Shui master would also be overjoyed to see a small rounded mound to the South, to embody the Palace of the Red Bird.

The Palace of the Green Dragon is in the East

The East is the direction of the sunrise, and in Chinese tradition is associated with springtime. It is also the palace of that most oriental of mythical animals, the dragon. This Eastern dragon is described as being azure or green due to the directional association with the Wood element, which is linked with these colours. Because of the identification with both the spring and the Wood element, the East is also associated with the growth of new shoots. Therefore, the energies arriving from the East bring a chi which is powerfully yang in nature, and is considered to be innovative and fertile. Like its opposite, the White Tiger, the Palace of the Green Dragon is thought of as a balance between the heat of the Red Bird and the cold of the Black Tortoise.

The Green Dragon is the symbolic animal of the East and of the element Wood. It is associated with springtime and the growth of new shoots. The chi arriving from the east is powerfully yang in nature.

The Palace of the Red Bird is in the South

The South is the direction most associated with the heat of high summer. The direction is described as the Palace of the Red Bird, variously identified with the mythical phoenix, a partridge or even a sparrow. Be that as it may, this direction is thought of as the most yang of all, its main expression being the element of Fire. The chi arriving from this direction will be warm, energetic, optimistic and extremely fortunate. However, due to the Chinese tradition of balance, it is held that too much of the good thing can be harmful, so care must be taken that the exuberant energies of the South do not overwhelm every other influence in the home. After all, warmth may be comforting, but too much heat will create nothing but a barren desert.

The Palace of the White Tiger is in the West

In contrast to the fertility and new life symbolized by the Green Dragon, the Palace of the White Tiger expresses endings, sunset and the season of autumn. The Tiger was regarded as a fearsome beast, unruly and unpredictable. The chi that comes from the West is stormy and disruptive, presiding over decrease and decay. The energies of the Tiger can create chaos if left unchecked (unless of course you happen to be a 6 or 7 Metal person (see page 27–28) in which case this wildness will actually work to your advantage). More generally, a barrier of some kind is placed to the West of the dwelling if that is the facing direction of the house or garden. However, if the facing direction happens to be to the North, then perhaps a shot of wild Tiger chi is just what you need to get your life and fortunes moving again.

The Phoenix or Red Bird is the symbolic animal of the south. It is associated with the height of summer. Its energies are fiery and extremely positive, but an over-emphasis on the southern quarter can create arid conditions in a garden.

The Palace of the Black Tortoise is in the North

The North is the direction of the Palace of the Black Tortoise and, as the name implies, its energies are slow, ponderous and sluggish. Even so, the North is considered the worst of the directions, bringing evil and misfortune down upon the home if it is not blocked in some way. This attitude may have a historical origin, since invasions of China have tended to come from that direction. This could also be the reason that the North is alternatively described as the Palace of the Black Warrior. Its element is Water (or in this case, ice) which, like a chilling glacier, freezes and spoils the fortunes of the household. Too much Tortoise chi can be very unlucky, but the balancing, calming yin energies of the North will be encouraged if your home faces South or West.

The slow moving Black Tortoise is associated with the wintry north. It is symbolic of the Water element and was distrusted by the ancient Feng Shui masters because they believed that evil tended to come from this quarter.

The White Tiger is symbolic of the West. This beast is considered to be wild and unruly. The Tiger is associated with the Metal element and the autumnal season.

The Eight Directional Trigrams

It really is impossible to over-emphasize how important the directions of the compass are in Feng Shui. It is no exaggeration to say that they are absolutely vital when one plans a home or a garden according to the ancient principles.

Now it is time to become acquainted with the Ba Gua, otherwise known as the Pa Kua. This is an arrangement of eight segments around a central point. It takes two forms called the Yin Ba Gua and the Yang Ba Gua.

The Yin Ba Gua

The Yin Ba Gua is placed on, or adjacent to, the principal doorway to the home to deflect 'secret arrows' and bad luck. The mirror is octagonal, each of its segments containing a figure made up of three lines. These three-line figures are called trigrams, and their constituent lines are broken or unbroken, or a combination of the two. An unbroken line symbolizes yang energy, while a broken line denotes yin energy. These trigrams derive from the ancient Chinese oracle manuscript, the *I Ching*, or Book of Changes.

The trigrams are arranged in an order called the Later Heaven sequence. This is thought to be passive in nature (hence the association with yin) and can deflect disruptive yang energy. It is important to ensure that when hanging a Ba Gua mirror the three

The Yang Ba Gua has the trigrams of the I Ching arranged in an order known as the 'Early Heaven' sequence. When used in conjunction with a small circular mirror in the centre, the three unbroken lines representing the trigram 'Ch'ien' should always be at the top.

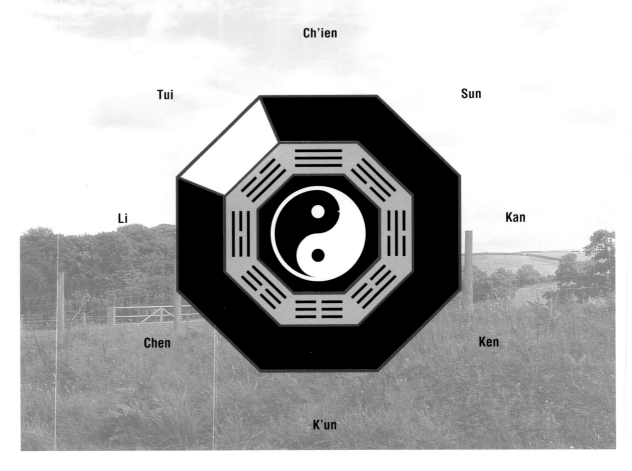

36

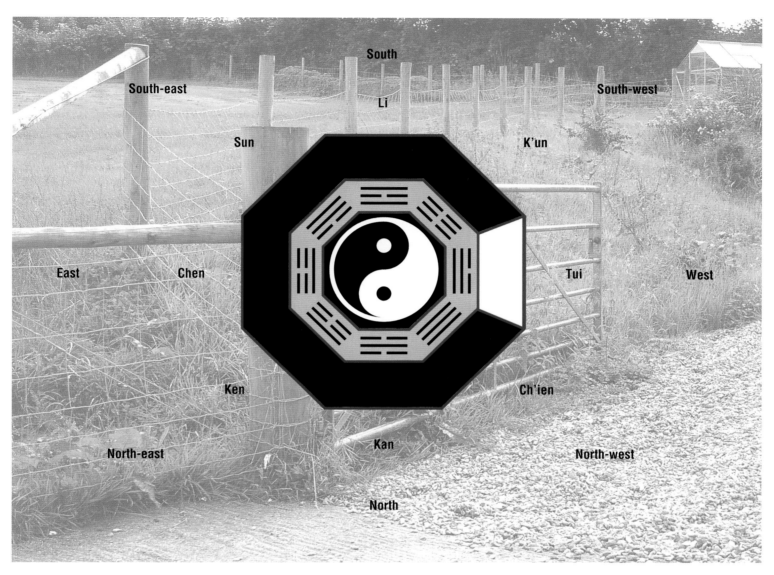

unbroken lines making up the trigram Ch'ien are at the top, and the three broken lines denoting the trigram K'un are at the bottom. Also, note that the Yin Ba Gua must only be displayed outside your home – never use it inside your dwelling as this is thought to deflect good fortune.

The Yang Ba Gua

This arrangement of trigrams forms the Early Heaven sequence, and it is used to allocate each of the trigrams to a compass direction beginning with the South, which we have already ascertained is associated with the Fire element and is located in the Palace of the Red Bird (see page 34). However, from the Yang Ba Gua we can see that the South is also associated with the trigram Li, which means 'the Flame'. Similarly, each of the compass directions has an independent interpretation according to the trigrams. These include family relationships, associated colours and of course the elemental bias which we have encountered before. In fact, you will notice that many of the symbols associated with the individual trigrams are the same as those associated with the Lo Shu Magic Square and the Star Numbers (see pages 16 and 22).

The Yin Ba Gua has the I Ching trigrams arranged in the 'Later Heaven' sequence. This arrangement provides a useful division of space since it allocates each trigram to a direction of the compass.

The South is Associated with the Trigram Li

The trigram Li which means 'Clarity' or 'the Flame' has many symbolic associations including the darting, flame-like goldfish, although usually not in this profusion.

Intimately connected with the Fire element and the Palace of the Red Bird, the trigram Li means 'The Flame' and 'The Clinging'. It symbolizes inspiration, clarity of mind, illumination and knowledge. Its main attribute is heat and is, therefore, associated with the height of summer. In Feng Shui tradition, Li is considered to be the best of the possible facing directions; however, this is not strictly true, since Water- and Metal-type people might well have difficulties with their main entrance facing an incompatible element. Be that as it may, a South-facing main doorway is eminently suitable for most other Star Numbers, especially for people born under 9 Fire. Creatures associated with the trigram are the phoenix, the pheasant or partridge, the sparrow and also the crab, shrimp, oyster, turtle and the humble goldfish. The family member symbolized by Li is the Middle Daughter and its associated colours are orange, wine-red and purple. The plants of the sector are those that tend to thrive in warm conditions or possess an inner heat of their own, such as tomatoes, chillies and peppers. Traditionally, trees in the southern part of a garden that are partly dried out are thought to be fortunate, as this shows that the heat of the South has touched them, but not damaged them. A high wall and gate in this direction should be a feature, too, since too much of Li's flame-like heat will whither your garden. Maintenance of this area in both the home and garden is important, because Li is said to influence the wellbeing of the eyes, the heart and the circulatory system.

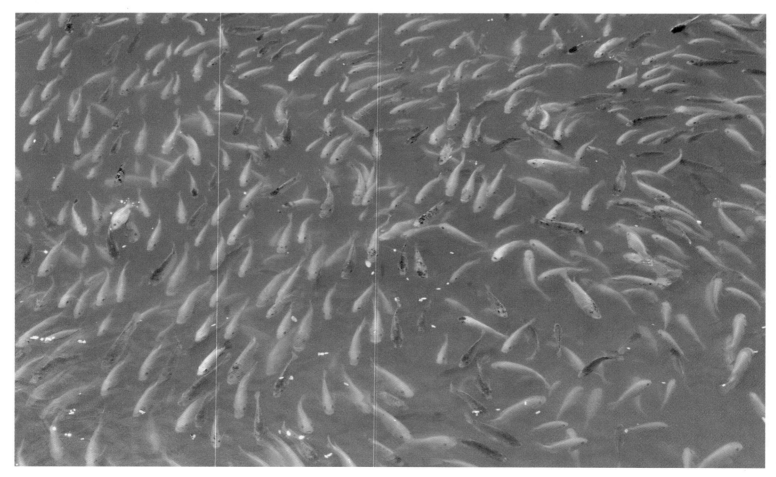

The South-west is Associated with the Trigram K'un

K'un is the most yin of the trigrams, and its symbol is made up of three broken lines. K'un is symbolic of the mother or the maternal influence in the household. Its name literally means 'Earth' and it forms the South-western portion of an earth axis which stretches through the centre to the North-eastern area of the trigram Ken. In terms of the body, K'un is associated with the stomach, as traditionally it was the duty of the mother to ensure that her family was fed. The nature of K'un is devoted and faithful, pure and charitable. It is also regarded as a fertile direction, so it is also symbolic of the womb. In keeping with the yin nature of the trigram, K'un is receptive, is acted upon rather than acting. Its colours are black and those of a dark hue, such as the rich brown of soil. The creatures associated with K'un are the hard-working ox, the breeding mare, the motherly cow and the ever-industrious ant. It is a favourable facing direction for women born under 5 Earth. In terms of the garden, this direction is connected to root vegetables such as potatoes, carrots, swede and parsnips. The association of K'un to roots leads to a connection with the past and with ancestral heritage. It is also symbolic of bulbs germinating in the fertile darkness of the earth.

K'un symbolizes the mother. It is also associated with the stomach and the provision of food. K'un is the south-western portion of the earth axis which stretches across the centre to the north-east.

The West is Associated with the Trigram Tui

The trigram Tui is symbolic of the smooth glassy surface of a placid lake. This trigram is metallic in nature just as the waters of the lake a reminiscent of a reflective sheet of metal or a mirror.

The name of this trigram means 'The Joyous' and 'The Lake'. It is calm and seemingly placid and, like a shiny metal plate, reflects heaven and earth. However, this tranquillity is deceptive because the lake has hidden depths. Likewise, the trigram refers to the depths of the psyche, with healing and also with magic. The nature of the trigram is joyful and rather sensual, suggesting an undercurrent of passion beneath a cool and inviting surface. This undercurrent of wildness is in keeping with Tui's placement in the area of the fearsome White Tiger. In terms of Feng Shui astrology, Tui is associated with 7 Metal and therefore it is suitable as a fortunate facing direction for those born under that number. Its symbolic season is the autumn or Fall and its auspicious colours are white and those of the setting sun or the russets and reds suggestive of falling leaves. Its symbolic animals include the sheep and the graceful antelope. In terms of the garden, plants considered fortunate here tend to like moisture, so anything that habitually grows by the shores of seas or lakes is favoured, as are trees like willows and mangroves. The direction of Tui is also considered to be an excellent place for a still, calming water feature. It has to be still, because an active one would stimulate the energies of the Tiger and bring disturbing feelings to the surface. The family relationship indicated by the trigram Tui is the Youngest Daughter.

The North-west is Associated with the Trigam Ch'ien

The word Ch'ien can be translated as 'The Creative' or 'Heaven' but as well as expressing the vault of the sky, it also indicates the head of the family or the father figure. This identification with the head of the household also means it is associated with the physical head and skull, and by extension of the idea to the mind and the thoughts within it. By nature, the trigram is strong and creative. It is extremely yang, its symbol being made up of three unbroken lines. The symbolic colours of Ch'ien are those of the Metal element, gold and white, and its associated animals are the Tiger of the West, the lion and the horse. The season attributed to Ch'ien is the late Fall or autumn, when the first flurries of snow are to be expected. The North-west is considered a particularly suitable facing direction for a 6 Metal person. This is certainly the case if that person also happens to be the head of the household, because it is to his or her health and fortunes that this area directly relates. In terms of the garden, the sector of Ch'ien is a good place to grow herbs. It is also suitable for fruit trees and chrysanthemums. Some Feng Shui experts suggest that it is a good idea to put a compost heap here because it is the perfect area for recycling, transforming the old and decaying into the new and fertile. This process is regarded as being the perfect expression of thought in terms of the landscape.

The trigram Ch'ien means 'Heaven' or the 'Creative'. It relates to the father figure, and like the whole of the western quarter, its main symbolic animal is the fierce tiger.

The North is Associated with the Trigram K'an

The most watery of the trigrams, it would be more correct to think of K'an as representing ice since it is located in the north.

K'an is considered to be an area of danger because it is found in the North. In Chinese history and tradition great disasters such as barbarian invasions, terrible storms and devastating plagues all seemed to originate in that direction. As might be imagined, K'an is associated with the biting cold of winter, so the trigram can be imagined as water in its frozen state as ice. The nature of the trigram is said to be frigid and treacherous; the cold of the North is of the kind that creeps into the bones and numbs the senses. There is an undercurrent of resentment about K'an, a jealousy which gnaws at the back of the mind, which may partly explain its association with the Middle Son in the household. A barrier in this direction is considered vital if ill-feeling is not to occur in the family. Nevertheless, the North is considered a good facing direction for a 1 Water person. For everyone else, the direction must be treated with some caution. In both home and garden it is a good place for an active water feature to stimulate the sluggish energies of the Black Tortoise. The plants associated with the area tend to be aquatic in nature and include reeds, bulrushes and water lilies. The willow, too, can be placed here in safety, because not only is it associated with riverbanks and pools, but it is said that it weeps for the tragedies of the past. The symbolic 'cold' colours of K'an are dark blue and black, silver and white, while its associated animals are the rat, pig, fox and bat.

The North-east is Associated with the Trigram Ken

The trigram Ken forms the North-eastern sector of the earth axis which stretches across the centre to K'un in the South-east. There are two translations of the name Ken, 'Mountain' and 'Keeping Still'. Just as its counterpart K'un sinks into the depths of the earth, the mighty Ken rears its rocky face high above it. Seemingly in defiance of its association with stillness, the trigram Ken symbolizes the Youngest Son. The animal imagery of Ken includes the dog, the mouse, the bull, ox and leopard. The North-west is the most favourable facing direction for men born under 5 Earth. The mountainous nature of Ken comes into its own in the garden because the North-east is the perfect site for a rock-ery which will provide a symbolic mound. This is particularly apt, since many alpine plants and heathers have a purple hue, and violet happens to be the associated colour of the trigram. Yellow and white are also associated colours. Feng Shui tradition would also hope for an old gnarled tree or a heavy boulder in this sector to suggest permanence. Traditionally, ranges of mountains are often described as being the 'backbone' of the country they occupy. The Rockies in the USA and the Pennines in England are examples of this. Likewise, the trigram symbolizes the spine and bone structure of a person. The hands, too, are thought to be influenced by this sector.

Ken symbolizes earth striving towards heaven and is represented by the craggy heights of mountains. It also provides the north-eastern portion of the earth axis which stretches from the south-west.

The East is Associated with the Trigram Chen

Chen is the area of the Eldest Son. It is located in the Palace of the Green Dragon of the East. Its name literally means 'Thunder' and it signifies explosive growth. In its symbolism Chen expresses a violent downpour which stimulates growth. It is also a fairly volatile influence, because thunderstorms can also cause flash floods and lightning strikes, which can be thought of as the fiery breath of the Green Dragon or the changeable moods of an adolescent. The season of the trigram, like that of the Palace it occupies, is the early springtime when all life is gaining strength and beginning to renew its vitality. This is the most suitable facing direction for those born with the Star Number 3 Wood. The symbolic colours of Chen are yellow, indigo and bright green and their combinations. The creatures associated with the trigram are the dragon, the eagle, cicada and swallow. In gardening terms, the Eastern sector is associated with sprouting shoots. It is thought that this direction is particularly good for evergreen trees and flower beds. In China, the sector of Chen is often reserved for the cultivation of the swift-growing bamboo. The body parts that are symbolically connected to Chen are the feet and also the throat and, by extension, the voice itself. Perhaps the thunder of Chen is suggestive of a teenager's breaking voice.

Chen, the trigram of the east is associated with abundant fertility. The colours of the springtime, such as green and vibrant yellow that are suggestive of growth, symbolize new life.

The South-east is Associated with the Trigram Sun

Sun, the name of this trigram can be translated in two ways. It can either literally mean 'Wood' or, more symbolically, 'The Gentle' referring to a light breeze moving through the leaves.

There are two possible translations of the word Sun. The first relates to the prevailing element of the direction, namely Wood. The second is 'The Gentle'. This seems to refer to the wind, or to be more accurate, a gentle breeze. It may also refer to a shoot bursting forth from the earth with surprising force. This trigram is said to be gentle and adaptable. It is symbolically associated with the dutiful Eldest Daughter and is connected with the concepts of perseverance, endurance, a sense of fair play and quiet determination. In ancient times, the eldest daughter of the household was expected to help raise the other children and was considered to be a fine catch in the marriage stakes. Thus she was left in no illusions that she was to be dutiful, come what may. The season of the trigram is early summer and it is the most favourable facing direction for those born under 4 Wood. The symbolic creatures associated with Sun include the cock, chicken, crane, snake, unicorn and earthworm. Its colour is a rich, dark green and the body parts that Sun is said to influence are the legs, lungs and gall bladder. In terms of the garden, the sector of Sun is the perfect place for a lawn or an unspoilt area of grassland. Lilies and poppies are considered to be auspicious flowers in this direction and tall trees of any type are also favoured.

The Fortunes of Your Home

Apart from their directional interpretations, studying the trigrams can reveal your fortunes in your home. Those who have a knowledge of the I Ching or Book of Changes, will already know that it consists of sixty-four hexagrams made up of a combination of two trigrams, one above and one below, symbolizing heaven and earth respectively. You may also remember that, with the exception of 5 Earth, most of the personal Star Numbers have an associated trigram. This will provide you with the upper, or heaven, trigram. The facing direction of your main entranceway will provide the lower or earth trigram. Put these together and you have a hexagram that reveals your destiny in your home. If you would like to interpret this hexagram or generally gain an overview of many aspects of Chinese mysticism, you can refer to one of the many available translations of the I Ching. I can also highly recommend *Chinese Divinations* by Sasha Fenton which clearly explains the often obscure aspects of oriental mystical thought (see the Bibliography).

Each of the Star Numbers is associated with one of the five elements of Wood, Fire, Earth, Metal and Water. It is also connected to one or more trigrams and a compass direction.

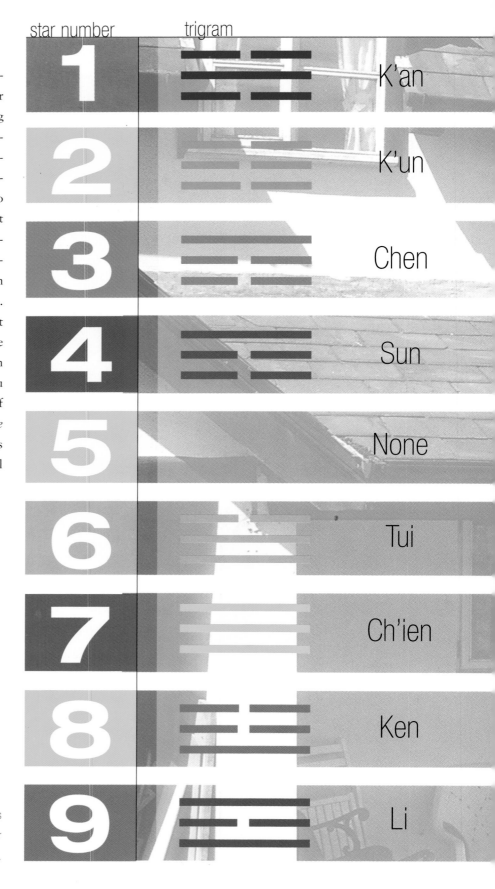

star number	trigram	
1		K'an
2		K'un
3		Chen
4		Sun
5		None
6		Tui
7		Ch'ien
8		Ken
9		Li

direction	meaning
north	water
south-west	earth / receptive
east	thunder
south-east	the gentle
centre	
west	the joyous / lake
north-west	heaven / creative
north-east	mountain / stillness
south	the flame / clinging

Putting it Together

By now you could be forgiven for thinking that with all these new concepts of lucky and unlucky directions, Star Numbers, symbolic animals and trigrams in a confusing jumble in your head that you'll never get the hang of Feng Shui. However, just follow the simple guidelines and take things one step at a time. Below is a reminder of what you need to do to get going with Feng Shui.

Note any areas that stick out or are missing, and then square off the whole plan with a dotted line to represent the missing portions. Now draw two faint lines from corner to corner to find the exact centre of your plan.

Still facing the front of your home, it will now become evident that the front door occupies one of three squares of the Lo Shu. These are 8 (front right from your position), 1 (the middle portion) or 6 (front left from your position). You are standing in square 5, so square 7 is to your immediate left, square 3 to your immediate right. The rest of the Lo Shu squares will now fall into place around your home. For the individual meaning of the Lo Shu squares, see pages 16–17.

Now take the directional compass and stand looking outwards from the front door. Take a directional reading from this position and mark it boldly on your floor plan. This is the facing direction and reveals the prevailing type of energy that enters your home as well as its ruling trigram and element.

Next, work out your personal Star Number which is based on the year of your birth. To do this, see the simple formula and table on pages 22 and 23. For the element, meanings and associations of each Star Number, see Feng Shui Astrology on page 22. When you have done this, you will know whether the direction of your main door and its ruling element are compatible with your fortunes or not according to

the table on page 23.

The listings under your personal Star Number will reveal those areas of your home that are compatible and harmonious with your fortunes. Likewise, there is also a list of those areas which are likely to be troublesome. For instance, if you were born in a 5 Earth year, the Lo Shu sectors which should be fortunate to you will be found in areas 9, 6 and 7 within your home. Sectors which are likely to cause misfortune are 1, 3 and 4, so you should take extra care in harmonizing the energies here.

To assess the Feng Shui of the garden, the process is very similar. Again, accurately mapping the area onto graph paper is the first step. Square off your diagram and fill in missing sections with a dotted line. Find the centre of the garden by drawing diagonal lines from corner to corner of your map. Standing at the centre with your compass, find the eight directions and allocate the trigrams. Then take a look at the surroundings to ascertain the facing direction and the type of chi that enters your garden (see Chi and the Symbolic Animals, page 30–35). If there is no obvious facing direction, then take this from the main entrance to the garden (see page 16). Bear in mind that your personal Star Number is irrelevant to exterior Feng Shui.

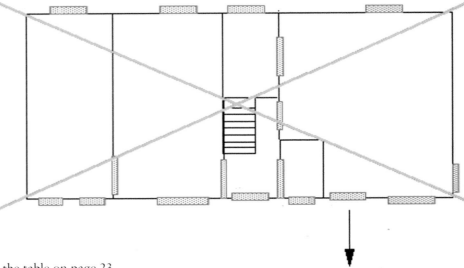

1 The first step is to draw a floor plan of your home on a piece of graph paper. This does not have to be 100 percent accurate, but you really should measure up to make sure that you are not too far off the mark. Draw in the doors, windows and other physical features of your home. If your abode is very irregular in shape such as an L-shape or even having 'wings' like an H, fill in the missing sectors with a dotted line.

2 Next, take an ordinary directional compass and, standing at the centre of your home (where the faint lines intersect), work out the cardinal directions of North, South, East and West as well as the intermediate directions such as north-east, south-west, etc. Mark these on your plan. Each direction indicates a trigram (see pages 36–45) and its symbols. Write the name of each trigram next to its direction.

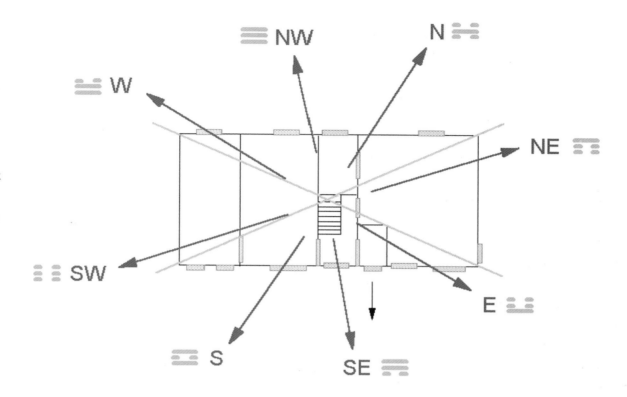

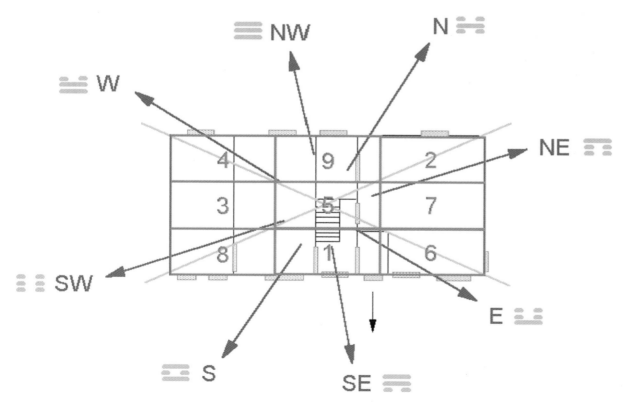

3 Still standing at the centre, face the front of your home (the wall that has the mainly used door in it). Now you can either use the Eight-point Method (see page 19), or make precision your goal by working out where the individual squares of The Lo Shu Magic Square diagram are located on your graph paper (see page 18). It is a good idea to use a different-coloured pen to annotate these.

the Front Door

The entrance to your home is a key area in Feng Shui, because it is through the front door that luck is likely to arrive, in the shape of visitors or mail. Of course, for reasons of convenience many people do not use the designated front door as their primary entrance. In some cases a side, garage or back door is used for this purpose. If this is so, then treat your usual access door as the main one.

In the traditions of Feng Shui, the front door is considered to be the 'mouth' of the house. Not only is sustenance taken through the mouth and into the physical system (symbolic of your living space) but it is also the organ of communication through which we interact with the outside world. Likewise the hallway that leads to the door can be considered to be the 'throat' of the dwelling.

Coping with Secret Arrows

The main doorway is also the area that is most sensitive to the attack of 'secret arrows'. These can be thought of as bolts of sha chi striking in straight lines, bringing ill-health and bad fortune in their wake, so care must be taken that these harbingers of doom are harmlessly deflected from your home.

To check for secret arrows, observation of your environment is important. First, stand at your front door, from the inside looking out, and scan the immediate area for sharp corners pointed directly at you. Then go around your home and look through all the windows. Secret arrows can manifest as a nearby lamp post or telegraph pole, or a satellite dish inclined in your direction. Anything sinister-looking such as a gargoyle or even a particularly ugly poster of a rock band in a neighbour's window can create a negative influence. However, the most noticeable creator of secret arrows will be a T-junction directly opposite your doorway. This allows negative sha chi to rush at your home, even if you live off a communal corridor.

If you do happen to have a doorway that opens

Calming Conflict

Here's how to resolve element conflict in your home by adding another element to calm warring forces.

When **WOOD** is in conflict with **EARTH**, resolve it with **FIRE**

When **FIRE** is in conflict with **METAL**, resolve it with **EARTH**

When **EARTH** is in conflict with **WATER**, resolve it with **METAL**

When **WATER** is in conflict with **FIRE**, resolve it with **WOOD**

When **WOOD** is in conflict with **METAL**, resolve it with **WATER**

The front of the house is East facing which is considered especially auspicious because David is governed by the Wood element, and the east is the direction of Wood. An uncluttered patio here is a must to ensure the good fortune from this direction. The garden itself is North facing so an active water feature visible from the front door would be a plus. This would be especially beneficial if a waterfall were included.

onto a communal passage, the attack of secret arrows is still a possibility. The proximity of an elevator or stairwell can cause negative influences to enter your living space.

If any of these secret arrow generators are present (and these days it is quite likely that they will be) you can use round-leaved, healthy plants on windowsills and outside your front door to diffuse the arrows. You can also fix a Ba Gua mirror (see page 55) to the door to deflect the negative energies. It is very important that the Ba Gua mirror should always face outwards, otherwise it might have the opposite effect of dispelling the positive energies already inside the dwelling, and you wouldn't want that to happen. If

the door has a glass panel then the mirror can be hung within, always remembering to make sure that it faces outwards and it is the right way up. The three unbroken lines describing the trigram Ch'ien (Heaven) should always be at the top, with the three broken lines making up the trigram K'un (Earth) at the bottom.

From experience, I can tell you that the effect of hanging up a Ba Gua mirror correctly has almost instant positive results. However, strictly speaking the use of the Ba Gua mirror is considered to be a fairly extreme measure because it will deflect the negative sha chi away from your home but possibly straight at someone else's. If you are concerned

about this possibility you could use a red coloured Chinese good-fortune symbol outside the door. These auspicious symbols take the form of Chinese characters and are generally available in Oriental stores around the world, particularly during Chinese New Year in late January or early February.

If it is impossible to fix the Ba Gua mirror to the door then it is permissible to hang it in a front window as close to the entrance as possible, and preferably at eye level. If neither of these options suits you then you could take a tip from a London restaurant owner who was shocked that her expensive prime

The sharp roofs of the shed and greenhouse point directly at the main door to the house creating secret arrows that can harm the fortunes of the inhabitants.

To prevent the secret arrows from penetrating the interior of the dwelling a scary mask, originally from the island of Bali, is placed by the door. In traditional Chinese thinking, this would serve to frighten away evil spirits. Fearsome items like this one should always face away from the house in case the friendly domestic spirits should take fright and flee the premises. In other cases a Ba Gua mirror would be placed on the door itself to achieve the purpose of deflecting secret arrows. On no account should the Ba Gua mirror face inwards.

Plants with spiky leaves should
be avoided.

Choose plants with rounded
leaves to enhance positive chi.

location premises was attracting few diners. After scanning the street outside, she noticed that two large and rather hideous stone gargoyles were leering at her and, moreover, pointed at the entrance to her restaurant from the rooftop of the building opposite. Since the lady did not run a Chinese eating establishment she felt that a Ba Gua mirror would be inappropriate in her case, so she opted for a very large, reflective brass doorknob to deflect the secret arrows coming her way from her lofty yet devilish neighbours. Since the doorknob was installed, business has picked up considerably. She later joked that the only problem that she had now was keeping the thing highly polished. The same technique might well work for you too.

The Direction of the Door

The direction of the main door to your home is vital to ascertain which kind of chi enters your dwelling. If, for instance, the doorway faces to South, then the type of energy encountered will be the fiery influence of the Red Bird. If West, then the disruptive force of the White Tiger will be the prevailing influence and so on (see page 34–35). This is equally true if you happen to live in an apartment, though the fact that there are two entrances (one personal to you and your family, the other for all the residents of the building) will inevitably complicate matters. In the case of apartments, the Feng Shui of your personal living space is paramount, although the position of your home within the more general Feng Shui layout of the building as a whole must also be considered.

Tradition also states that the approach to the main entrance should be via a gentle, meandering path to avoid the danger of sha chi, which likes to take the straight and narrow path. A curved approach to the house is thought to increase the income potential of those who live within. It is advised that the front of the property should be defined by a low wall. It is also recommended that a

pond or other water feature should be prominent near the entrance (preferably to the left of the doorway). Fortunately, none of the above is strictly necessary which is a good thing as so many of us live off busy streets or communal hallways. The front door itself should be a fairly solid construction to protect your property and, although glass is one of the materials favoured by traditional Feng Shui, its use in the main door to your home should ideally be limited.

The Star Number Directions

It is easy to work out if a certain property will be a happy environment for you and promote good luck, health and prosperity by use of your elemental Star Number (see pages 22–23 to ascertain which elements and directions are most fortunate for you). As previously stated, the Star Number brings with it many associations with colours, shapes and most

The Ba Gua mirror should always face away from the dwelling and care should be taken that the three unbroken lines representing the trigram Ch'ien are at the top. The mirror is a powerful tool used to deflect troublesome secret arrows.

The water-barrel, which is not particularly aesthetically pleasing, has a useful Feng Shui function in providing a water feature to the garden which would otherwise be missing. Since this garden is North facing a more active water feature would be better to stimulate the slow moving chi.

importantly in this case, good and bad directions. Below is a table of lucky and unlucky directions for the main entrance to your home. You will notice that the worst directions given are the opposite ones to the best; however, this does not work in quite the same way for directions that are ruled by the Earth element. The reason for this is that the Earth element essentially governs the centre of anything, and therefore it cannot be said to have a facing direction. However, because of the compatibility with both the North-east and the South-west, it can be said to express an 'axis'.

In an ideal world everyone would have a doorway that points in their best direction, but its important to remember that these are guidelines only because there are other directions given in the main table that can be fortunate, or at least neutral, for you.

However, if you do not live alone, there could be another complication. Perhaps a direction that is potentially lucky for you has quite the opposite effect for your partner. In this circumstance a compromise must be found that avoids the worst possible directional influences for both parties.

Harmonious Door Colours

If, however, you are faced with the problem that your front door direction is unfortunate for either your or your partner, all is not lost. You can always use colour as a Feng Shui cure for this inauspicious placement. The colour you choose should be in harmony with your Star Number. For instance, if your number is 7, this corresponds to the Metal element, therefore white should be used. If you have a Star Number of 5, governed by the Earth element, think

Star Number and Element	Best Direction	Next Best	Worst
1 Water	North	South-east	South
2 Earth	South-west	North-east	South-east
3 Wood	East	South	West
4 Wood	South-east	North	North-west
5 Earth (males)	North-east	South-west	North & East
5 Earth (females)	South-west	North-east	South-east
6 Metal	West	North-west	East
7 Metal	North-west	West	South-east
8 Earth	North-east	South-west	North & East
9 Fire	South	East	North

about yellow or muted earthy shades to transform the influences of an unlucky direction into a more positive influence on your life. The same holds true if you are in a partnership. According to the creation cycle of elements (see page 12) Earth creates Metal, so both are in harmony. Therefore, either white or yellow can be used to paint the front door. If however, an 8 Metal person has teamed up with a 9 Fire person, problems can occur so consult the table of elemental conflicts on page 13 to find a compatible resolution. In the case of a Fire and Metal conflict, the resolution lies in the Earth element, so a suitable colour would again be yellow or muted earthy tones.

Using Feng Shui Symbols

One can further increase good fortune by placing certain symbolic images or objects near the front door. If you have a front garden, consider siting ornamental dragons lions on either side of the door to ward off 'evil spirits'. These can also be placed in windows for the same effect. Make sure that these fearsome beasts face away from the house, because if they face inwards they will frighten away the benign influences in the home. If your main door faces West or you are a ruled by the Metal element according to your Star Number, then you might consider hanging a picture of a tiger just inside the door. Of course, the tiger should be facing the door to scare off the sha chi.

A wind chime in a porch or just within the door will also promote good chi, though a little care and thought taken over the materials that the chime is made of will avoid any potential elemental conflicts. So ensure that you only use a metal chime in a Metal or water direction. Wood is a suitable material in the East, and you can use a pinkish or red glass wind chime in the South. Tradition holds that a bamboo flute placed just within the door will dispel negative energies because in the Cantonese language the word for 'flute' sounds like the word 'disappear'.

The ever popular temple dogs (also inaccurately called dragons or lions) should never face into the house from a doorway or windowsill. Their original function was to frighten away evil spirits and bad luck so if you possess a pair of these fearsome beasts face them outwards and watch your luck change for the better.
The male dog is the one with the pearl of wisdom under his foot, while the female guards a small cub

The use of windchimes are a feature of Feng Shui. The movement of air past them causes them to ring or to move gently and this actually creates chi. They are therefore useful in areas where there is little or stagnant chi. Traditionally, wind-chimes can deflect secret arrows and transform a negative area into a positive one.

If You Don't Succeed...

If you are still experiencing bad luck after following the advice above, and believe in your heart of hearts that the cause is the sha chi gushing through the main door, then the only option left is to block off the offending entrance and use another one if at all practical. However, this is a last resort, so do persevere with other Feng Shui remedies first.

the Hallway

Let's begin with a worst-case scenario. If you stand at the front door looking into your house, is there a through-passage that leads directly to the back door? If so, the dreaded sha chi will be attracted by the straight lines of this space, and tend to race through your home, not stopping to allow any of more positive influences to linger. Ancient Chinese emphasizes that nothing but bad luck can come of living in a house with such an obvious wind-tunnel effect. The same might be said if the main door and a window directly align along a passageway. However, there are simple remedies that, although they may not cure the situation, can at least slow down the progress of chi through your home.

Patterned rugs, especially if they have swirling designs on them can slow down chi down most effectively and transform negative sha into positive sheng. A small, semi-circular table placed midway in the hall will have a similar effect. Healthy plants can be used, too. A plant with rounded leaves, such as a money tree, is preferable to one that has a spiky appearance. This spikiness obviously includes plants such as cacti. Also, do not display cut flowers here because they represent 'dead' energy, and roses with thorns are therefore particularly unhelpful in the battle against sha chi.

Windchimes at each end of the hall (remembering to take account of the elemental bias of the directions) will help too. One remedy that I have found to be particularly efficacious is the placement of a series of small mirrors at eye level on one wall of the hallway reflecting a large mirror or joyous picture on

Calming Conflict

Here's how to resolve element conflict in your home by adding another element to calm warring forces.

When **WOOD** is in conflict with **EARTH**, resolve it with **FIRE**

When **FIRE** is in conflict with **METAL**, resolve it with **EARTH**

When **EARTH** is in conflict with **WATER**, resolve it with **METAL**

When **WATER** is in conflict with **FIRE**, resolve it with **WOOD**

When **WOOD** is in conflict with **METAL**, resolve it with **WATER**

the other. The mirrors cause the chi to bounce back and forth along the length of the hall, thereby slowing it down and forcing it to meander through your property. (Take care that you don't actually place a mirror at the head or foot of the stairs, because this is said to promote accidents - see page 67). Another remedy is to create a psychological doorway within the passage. You can use a bead curtain, especially one with reflective beads, if this suits your taste.

Of course, most hallways do not extend along the entire length of the home, but even so any long, straight area will encourage the negative effects of sha chi, so some of the Feng Shui remedies given

ABOVE: The dragon-boat of the eight gods of happiness is actually a Japanese symbol but nonetheless represents many good things entering your home and your life. The eight gods were said to voyage around the world distributing their gifts of longevity, jollity, love, intelligence, luck, money, children and success in examinations. The symbol of the dragon-boat cannot fail to be auspicious.

RIGHT: This beautiful carved ornament is ideally suited for a windowsill. Its colour makes it particularly suitable for water areas.

above will prove useful in dealing with this portion of your home.

Colour and Light

Hallways should be painted in a light, uplifting colour because this is by nature yang, or active. Sombre, gloomy hallways are neither conducive to good fortune nor good moods. So, the main entrance should not open into a narrow or constricted hall because these areas tend to be dark, restricting the flow of chi into the home. The main impression should be of an area that is light and airy, so if your hallway is a twilight zone, think about using bright

LEFT: This extremely beautiful piece of oriental craftsmanship is a particularly suitable decoration for the Wood area of the home. It might also be used where a conflict between the elements Fire and Water is a danger to family fortunes.

BELOW: Long, straight corridors encourage chi to move too swiftly to leave any fortunate benefits. Particularly long passageways need special attention. Otherwise, even positive chi becomes too charged with energy and can act like a secret arrow by the time it reaches the end of the passage.

LEFT: Seen from this angle, the reflective effects of using mirrors to break up a long, narrow space are clearly visible.

ABOVE: Mirrors or attractive pictures can help in slowing down chi that is too swift.

A large mirror placed on a wall opposite a series of smaller ones causes the chi to 'bounce' along the length of the corridor.

colour here, and bring in spot lighting to illuminate any dark corners.

Some traditions also state that the first thing that one sees when entering will have a bearing upon the fortunes of the occupants. Therefore, it is a good idea to include something beautiful in your decoration scheme. This can be a lovely painting, a gorgeously patterned rug or an elegant urn, or indeed anything else that pleases your taste and eye. Just remember that proportion is important in Feng Shui, so don't defeat the purpose of the exercise by putting anything too large in your hallway - no matter how beautiful you consider it to be. After all, if it is so wonderful, it should easily fit into an alternative space.

As with all the practices of Feng Shui, it is your instinct and sense of proportion that are the most important factors. If you think that you have pleasing surroundings then the chances are that you have instinctively got the Feng Shui right in the first place. If not, then try out some of the traditional remedies presented here until you have achieved the perfect hallway.

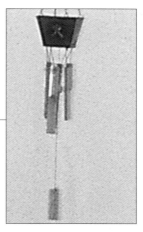

ABOVE: A windchime would be a useful addition to any long passageway. Movement which causes it to chime is auspicious.

ABOVE: A series of small mirrors will slow down chi along a passageway.

The curved contours of this day-bed will help to transform harmful sha chi into the more harmonious sheng chi.

When dealing with a long straight corridor it is a good idea to place a series of small mirrors along one wall. A larger mirror or a picture of a pleasing scene can be hung on the wall opposite. This has the effect of causing the chi to bounce back and forth, effectively slowing down its momentum and allowing it to distribute its benefits. Since this hallway is wide an arrangement of furniture along one side is also auspicious. The curved sofa or day-bed is a particularly good feature. An alternative treatment, effective in a narrower space would be a long rug with swirling patterns to further hamper the swift chi.

In the case of David and Sarah's home the bottom of the stairs is located at the very centre of the house. In Feng Shui, the centre of anything relates to the Earth element and the health of the occupants. To ensure that the chi flow here is beneficial a windchime has been hung at the precise centre.

The Stairway

Strictly speaking, the traditions of Feng Shui disapprove of a stairway that directly faces the front door. However, here in the unenlightened Western world we have grown used to such an arrangement as a standard feature in many of our homes. The situation would be made worse if the stairs aligned with the main entrance from the end of a long hallway. In this case the remedies that apply to the hall such as patterned rugs, the use of wind chimes, mirrors, round tables and plants to slow down and dispel sha chi are of extra importance. You can also use a divider to screen off the door area, provided that you have enough space at the bottom of the hall and it does not obstruct your movement. Another solution is to hang a spider plant or other decorative foliage in basket from the ceiling. Although a spider plant does have pointed leaves, the overall shape of the plant is curved, creating the roundness that promotes good chi and, in this case, acts as a symbolic screen between the front door and the stairs.

The rules for the stairs themselves are generally dictated by common sense. A banister and handrails are recommended; secure carpeting and a lack of clutter are a necessity. However, there are some principles that are unique to the practice of Feng Shui. The use of mirrors in a stairwell should be limited, and do not hang mirrors at the top and at the foot of the stairs. Mirrors here can be disorienting and are said to cause accidents.

A staircase with gaps between the runners is not a good idea either because the chi is thought to seep through the stairs and never reach the upper floor at all. However, if you do have an open staircase then a healthy plant placed beneath it will encourage the positive energies to ascend, as will a light or an active aquarium.

As good Feng Shui prefers curves to straight lines, it is surprising that an attractive feature like a spiral staircase is not considered conducive to good for-

Mirrors placed at the head or foot of the stairs are bad Feng Shui. Not only do they dissipate the chi, but traditionally speaking they are said to promote accidents. From a practical point of view too, mirrors can also be a safety hazard, distracting the eye just at the moment when one's attention should be focused on placing one's feet with care

tune. If you do possess a spiral staircase then the only way to increase the sheng chi is to ensure that it is well lit. Surrounding the area with healthy plants with exuberant foliage will also help.

Quick Tips

- Check for secret arrows (see page 52) and remedy with plants, wind chimes, bamboo flutes, auspicious symbols or, in extreme cases, the Ba Gua mirror
- Check the direction of your front door and its compatibility with the elements of your Star Number (see page 57)
- Choose colours that support the associated elements (see page 57–8)
- Slow down negative chi with a patterned rug, small tables, plants and wind chimes if your stairs, or another door, face the front door
- Use mirrors along long, dark hallways to increase positive chi
- Do not place mirrors at the foot or at the top of stairs

the Living Room

The living room can be considered to be the heart of the house. It is the room where you will spend most of your time when at home, and it should reflect not only your own tastes and character, but also provide a haven of comfort and tranquillity. The importance of aesthetically pleasing living space cannot be overstated. It is here that you will tend to entertain visitors to your home, so it needs to be welcoming to others. It should also be noted that this is the room that provides the space for cherished personal possessions and mementos as well as housing your sofa, chairs, hi-fi and television.

The living room is a strongly yang area of the home, therefore your choice of decoration should reflect some yin to ensure the correct Feng Shui balance. Soft furnishings, plenty of cushions, some lush, healthy plants (without thorns or spiky leaves) or a tank with goldfish will help to ensure a pleasing appearance and a pleasant atmosphere.

Using the Lo Shu Magic Square

It is in the living room that the use of the Lo Shu Magic Square comes into its own. This room should be assessed quite separately from the rest of the house. The furnishings should be placed with care according to the nine divisions of the Lo Shu.

First, stand at the entrance to the living room, looking inwards. The corner to your far right is the relationships area (area 2 in the Lo Shu) which in terms of the lounge can be thought of as the 'power corner'. This is the probably the best place to put your electronic equipment, hi-fi, television and other mass media paraphernalia. Remember, this area is also dedicated to those you love, so displaying a photograph or treasured gift from those who mean the most to you will be fortuitous.

In the living room, three other Lo Shu areas are vitally important. These are areas 4, 5 and 6, which

4	9	2
3	5	7
8	1	6

The Lo Shu Magic Square has relevance to the layout of a living room. This diagram should be made separately while bearing in mind the location of the lounge within the home as a whole.

corner is in a Metal or Water direction, then this is a good place for a fish tank or some decorative oriental coins, which can be purchased from Chinese stores. You can tie together three coins, or multiples of three, with red cord or ribbon to activate their wealth-bringing luck. You can also place pebbles or other attractive stones on a gold plate to symbolize money.

If the prevailing direction of the corner is East, relating to the Wood element then a healthy plant is a good idea. If this corner lies to the South then a lamp or a red ornament would serve to represent Fire. Of course, you could also use one of the symbolic images associated with one of the eight directional trigrams to ensure the prosperity of the household (see pages 38-45). For example, a picture of a mountain would suit the trigram Ken, or an image of a lake for the trigram Tui.

are associated with money, health and friendships respectively. These areas form a diagonal from the far left to the near right corners of the room, from the perspective of the doorway.

Area 4, which relates to money, lies in the far-left corner of the room. It needs to have a symbolic item in it that is in harmony with its direction and element, and which also represents prosperity. If this

Area 5 is at the exact centre of the room. It relates to the Earth element and it is associated with the health and physical wellbeing of you and your family. Ideally, this area should be left as plain as possible.

The relationship area of the living room is the furthest left-hand corner from the mainly used entrance to that room. This is also considered to be a 'power corner' so it is a suitable place for videos, hi-fis and the tv. However it shouldn't be forgotten that it does relate to your personal relationships, so a few personal photos or mementos of loved ones here is a good idea.

The earth axis runs through the centre of any space from the north-east to the south-west. The colour blue is not recommended anywhere along this axis, neither is anything that has water as its theme. According to the Destruction Cycle of the elements, earth pollutes water so this could damage the luck of the household. The photograph illustrates the south-eastern portion of David and Sarah's living room which is also the area of prosperity. Cash flow is likely to be harmed by suggesting water in such an earthy area.

A stirring sea-scape would be auspicious in a Water ruled area, but it has a negative effect along the earth axis which runs from the south-west to the north-east.

This image of a ship is also misplaced in an earth ruled area.

ABOVE: This blue/green coloured ornament places it as a 'watery' object.

Again, blue items suggestive of water are inauspicious here.

No special symbolism is necessary here, simply because the very centre of the room should be left uncluttered to facilitate ease of movement. However, if you really must have a coffee table placed in the middle, its shape should be dictated by the shape of the room. A rectangular living room, for example, calls for a rectangular or oval coffee table. Likewise, in a room that is square a circular or octagonal table should be chosen. Whatever the shape of the table, it is vital to ensure that it is not constantly messy. In terms of the family's health, a table continually covered in old newspapers, magazines, ashtrays and used coffee cups is not going to do your nearest and dearest any good at all.

Area 6 is associated with friendships, helpful people, allies and spiritual benefits. It is sited at the near right-hand corner from the viewpoint of the doorway. As well as being the obvious place for seating

The addition of gold hued cushions in an earth area is good Feng Shui.

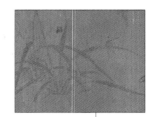

The main colour of gold in this painting is extremely auspicious in an earth-ruled sector.

Ornaments suggestive of the sun are harmonious in this area for two reasons. First, the sun is of the Fire element and Fire creates Earth. Secondly, the object itself is made of metal and Earth creates Metal. It is also yellow, the symbolic colour of the Earth element. This is a good example of the Creation Cycle in action.

A better arrangement of the south-eastern sector of David and Sarah's living room includes a golden theme. This suggests the element Metal and according to the Creation Cycle of the elements, Earth creates Metal, so prosperity should now be enhanced. The fact that the prevailing colour is gold should be beneficial for the financial fortunes too. The shiny pebbles arranged on a square dish is a nice touch. Pebbles are things of the earth, square is the shape symbolic of the earth element and the golden colour suggests both Metal and prosperity.

The other end of the earth axis is the north-east. A cluttered environment here, with dull colours and items symbolic of the water element are unwelcome suggesting a loss of direction and self doubt.

This area is governed by earth, so water-based objects are bad.

Any disorderly piles of papers or other clutter is bound to cause sha chi in neglected corners.

Although no one wants to live in a state of clinical organisation, it is wise to tidy up a little.

A little mess is acceptable as long as you don't allow it to hang around for too long.

The north-eastern corner of the living room will be considerably improved by the addition of gold and black cushions, the colours of Metal and Earth. The sun mirror is a pleasing touch suggesting light and prosperity. Its inclusion enlivens a section of the wall which was neutral. Keeping this area free of clutter will promote mental clarity.

arrangements, if you want to keep on good terms with your friends, this is also the ideal area for the telephone. This will ensure that you are the recipient of happy news.

As well as referring to friendships and helpful people, area 6 is also traditionally connected to the

The heavy beam which bisects the living room is an obvious feature that needs a Feng Shui cure or two to prevent its symbolic weight resting on the shoulders of the inhabitants. The Northern end of the beam is in the North, the Water direction so a black wind-chime here helps to lighten the load. Since this is the Water area, a goldfish bowl or a more elaborate aquarium directly beneath this end of the beam would be a very auspicious addition to the room.

gods, or the helpful forces of the universe. This means that it is also a good location for items that have a spiritual or symbolic significance, such as a rosary or a statuette of the Buddha. Icons such as these tend to serve a dual purpose in that they lead the mind to ponder spiritual truths and at the same time provide a conversation piece, which is perfect for this most convivial of areas.

Danger points

The arrangement of a living room does present certain difficulties, which can have a negative effect on family fortunes if they are not addressed. Begin by assessing the position of chairs and sofas. Chairs

Black and gold objects are auspicious in an area governed by wood. Space clear of clutter promotes positive chi.

The gold framed mirror is an idea object to fill the blank wall.

Again, the addition of cushions in favourable colours is good Feng Shui.

The fireplace is in the Fire sector of the living room which is not only fortunate but also very practical. The fire-guard is a must not only from the point of view of child safety, preventing accidents but also deterring positive chi from escaping up the chimney. The fiery symbolism is continued even on warm days by the inclusion of candles on the grate

should not be placed with their backs facing the doorway to the room, or if the lounge is open plan, backing onto another sector of the home. This form of seating arrangement, although it may appear comfortable, will only serve to project unwanted sha chi into the adjoining area. Likewise chairs, especially that typically used by the head of the household, should not back onto a window or be placed under a heavy beam. This type of chair placement creates an unconscious sense of unease that will eventually manifest as outright anxiety and soaring stress levels.

An open fireplace can also create problems. Although Fire creates positive chi, a chimney will tend to draw energy from the room. Therefore, if the fireplace is in a good location according to the Lo Shu Magic Square, it is a good idea to place a mirror above the fireplace to deflect the chi back into the room. If you do choose this option, remember that a fire guard is a necessity, not just because it creates a useful Feng Shui barrier but, more importantly, because many accidents have been caused by people tip-toeing to see their reflection in front of a blaze. As usual common sense in this, as in any other Feng Shui remedy should be the paramount concern. If the fireplace is in a troublesome sector then the mirror option is definitely out because it will only serve to help positive chi escape.

Ideally, the main entrance to the living room should not be aligned with the window. If this is difficult to arrange, try Feng Shui cures such as wind chimes and plants (see also the Front Door and Hallway, pages 50–67). However, in this case an occa-

The attractive, smooth pebbles on a square, golden dish symbolise health and prosperity. The pebbles themselves are earthy in nature as indeed is the shape of their container. The gold, or Metal component is in harmony with Earth being created from that element. This attractive item would be particularly beneficial at the centre of the house or in the 'money area' to ensure material success.

The placement of the sofa with its back to the window is bad Feng Shui. Sitting here for any length of time will promote feelings of anxiety and possibly cause depression. However, in this room there is little alternative because of the sofa's size. It still isn't good, but there is one mitigating factor in that the window faces the east, the direction of the Green Dragon, and that is David's fortunate direction so things are not as bad as they might be. The green grass outside, the good view and the ornaments of the windowsill will also help.

sional table set between the two will usually suffice, especially if it is left uncluttered.

Perfect arrangement

Having set out the potential problems, it is reassuring to note that arranging the living room to perfection is not difficult if you follow the simple rules. A stress-free environment depends on good communication, bringing relaxation. The best way to achieve a calm interchange of views is to put some thought into the location of chairs and sofas. You can create a harmonious seating arrangement by placing two chairs and the sofa at a slight angle to each other, but not directly opposite. This arrangement will provide open conversation without appearing to be too confrontational as would be the case if the seats face each other directly.

An arrangement of seats in the shape of a horseshoe is said to be the best and the most fortunate. If you are planning to arrange your seating in this way, check that none of the chairs backs onto an adjoining room. This will only minimize the positive effect of the horseshoe.

If you have no option but to place a sofa under a window, you can activate other positive features to minimize the effect. If, for example, the window looks onto the green dragon area of your garden (see page 33), you can symbolically strengthen his protective influence by placing green ornaments on the window ledge.

Wherever possible, chairs and sofas should be positioned with their backs to a wall. Again, the rule against positioning the backs of seats against doors or windows comes into play because this will cause the sitter to feel psychologically vulnerable.

If your living room has doors that oppose each other across the length of the room try not to arrange the seating with one chair on one side of line of the doors, with the others occupying the other side. This situation will only led to one member of the family being symbolically excluded and make them feel isolated and lacking in self-esteem. This is a situation that the Feng Shui masters claim will lead to explosive outbursts of temper and consequent family disharmony.

Exposed beams are frowned upon, and particularly so in such an important part of the home as the living room. It is said that sitting directly beneath an exposed ceiling beam will lead to depression and feelings of despondency. Ideally, it is better to move chairs and sofas away from beams if at all possible, then apply Feng Shui cures to the beams themselves. You can use a bamboo flute, preferably hung an angle of 45 degrees, to dispel the oppressive influence of the beam. Apart from its Chinese symbolism as a dispeller of evil, by its very nature the flute also suggests a certain airiness within the room. A mobile or wind chime fulfils the same function, especially if it is positioned directly above the afflicted seating area.

All of the above rules about seating become more important when considering the position of the chair of the head of the household. As well as making sure that he or she does not sit under a beam or with their backs to a window or an adjoining room, Feng Shui tradition also states that he or she should face their most fortunate direction (see the Star Number profiles on pages 22-23). This encourages the positive chi to infuse the body and increase health and vigour.

Good Proportions

Remember that the essence of Feng Shui is that everything should be in proportion, therefore the furniture you choose should not be either too big or too small for the room. If your furniture is over-sized then the living room will be cramped and uncomfortable. The positive energies of sheng chi will be hampered, and family fortunes will suffer. Your options will be reduced as the open space in the living room is reduced. On the other hand, if the furniture is too small, your options may be open but you

The other end of the beam lies in the southern sector of the room. This of course if the Fire area. A windchime made of crystal beads is a good idea here because it not only serves to lighten the load of the beam, psychologically speaking but also reflects the glorious light of the South.

will lack the will to take advantage of them, and you may start to dwell on the deficiencies of life, rather than the opportunities that are presented to you.

Before we leave the living room, there is one final point to take into account. An East- or South-facing lounge is particularly suitable for the type of person who likes to rise early, take full advantage of the day and live a healthy lifestyle. It is also beneficial to those who are artistic or creative in some other way. A living room that faces West or North is more likely to appeal to those who love to talk and laugh over a glass or two of wine way into the wee small hours of the morning.

Quick Tips

- Go for healthy, round-leaved plants to encourage chi and deflect secret arrows
- Cushions and throws supply yin energy to balance the natural yang of the living room and give a feeling of comfort
- Go for a horseshoe seating arrangement for security and good family fortune
- Calming pictures are conducive to good communication
- Clearing up cluttered coffee tables will help neutralize irritation between family members

the Dining Area

From ancient China to the present day, it has been believed that the process of eating provides nourishment not only for the body, but also for the spirit. Consequently, the Feng Shui view is that being distracted while eating will cause disharmony, ill-health and generally disrupt the smooth running of the household. Of course, this also means that having a snack on a tray while glued to the television is terrible for your chi.

Ideally, you should have a dining room, but in many homes space does not allow for this, and we often eat in a designated area of the kitchen or living room. If this is the case, you will need to define the dining area by using a screen as a room divider. Traditionally, this is considered to be the best option, because it is more likely to prevent distraction than using, say, a sideboard or a sofa for this purpose. Healthy plants can also act as a symbolic screen – they bring in calming chi, creating a peaceful atmosphere in the dining area. Remember to choose plants with rounded leaves.

A dining area that is too close to the main entrance to the home is not thought to be good Feng Shui. This would mean that the family's eating area is too accessible and will attract disturbance, promote gluttony and generally reduce the hospitality of the home.

Table Shapes and Seating

The main focus of the dining area is the dining table. Loud patterns and glaring colours in this room count as a distraction, and are not encouraged. You should not be overwhelmed by your surroundings when you are eating a meal.

Choose a circular or octagonal table, because this is considered to be more fortunate and conducive to family harmony than a square or rectangular one. (This is also sensible from a safety point of view, especially when one has small children, as it is easier to bruise oneself against a corner than against a curve.) In Feng Shui, corners within the dining room are thought to cast secret arrows, which cause digestive problems and irritations. It is particularly important that no one is seated directly at the corner of the dining table no matter how crowded your dinner parties become.

Calming Conflict

Here's how to resolve element conflict in your home by adding another element to calm warring forces.

When **WOOD** is in conflict with **EARTH**, resolve it with **FIRE**

When **FIRE** is in conflict with **METAL**, resolve it with **EARTH**

When **EARTH** is in conflict with **WATER**, resolve it with **METAL**

When **WATER** is in conflict with **FIRE**, resolve it with **WOOD**

When **WOOD** is in conflict with **METAL**, resolve it with **WATER**

A dining area should have an atmosphere of calm and tranquillity. In this case, the chances of a little peace in which one can consume food is limited to say the least. The heavy beam above the table would make one anxious and unsettled. The busy tablecloth and the cluttered sideboard do not make for a tranquil mind. In addition, the bare lightbulb creates sha chi.

Clutter on a dining table in the centre of the room could adversely affect health.

A patterned table cloth is not conducive to mental calm or good digestion.

A bare light bulb is bad Feng Shui because any glare is a form of secret arrow.

Piles of neglected paper are thought to be sha chi generators.

Dried flowers are not recommended anywhere in the home, and the same applies to pot pourri. These after all are dead, and indeed symbolize death and bad luck generally. The Feng Shui advice on pot pourri is to get rid of it as quickly as possible.

Good Table Decoration

Begin by removing tablecloths with garish, distracting patterns and choose one in a plain, calming colour. White is good, as are pale blue and green and other pastels — these are calming yin shades.

Next, you need to consider the table decoration. Bearing in mind that proportion is key in Feng Shui, a decorative arrangement should not be too large, too busy or too distracting to the diners. Although dried flowers are popular, they are not good, as Feng Shui frowns on anything in the home that is lifeless. Desiccated plants (and grasses or pot pourri) symbolize death to the oriental mind, which is not particularly conducive to happy thoughts.

There is also a disapproval of cut flowers in a vase, no matter how pretty they might be, because again they represent bad energy and dying. Flowers in bloom are also symbolic of the end of life, since by their very nature they are impermanent.

Good solutions for a table centrepiece are candles in attractive candle holders. Choose the colour of your candles and the material of the holders in accordance with the creative cycle of elements (see page 12). For example, for a Fire room you could choose green candles in wooden holders to symbolize the element of Wood, which feeds fire. If your dining table is at the very centre of your dining room, use candles in metal holders. This is because the cen-

Light shades should prevent the misfortune generated by glare.

A healthy plant will prevent a build up of sha chi.

A plain tablecloth promotes a calm and contemplative frame of mind as does the tranquil, pastoral scene in the painting. The bushy plant creates positive chi while the wind-chime on the beam serves to lift its weight from the minds of the diners. The table's centrepiece, the candles reflects the Fire element which creates the Earth element. Since the table is the centre of the dining area the combination of Fire and Earth here is beneficial to health, most particularly the digestion.

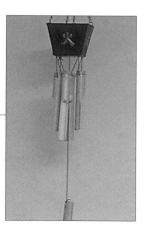

A windchime will lift the heavy weight of the beam.

tre is the Earth area and in the creation cycle of elements Fire (the candles) creates Earth, which in turn creates Metal (the candle holders). This creative interplay of elemental forces will enhance the positive sheng chi of the area very well.

Chairs for Good Chi

Curves are preferable for the dining chairs, too. They should also be comfortable so that you will actually enjoy sitting in them, rather than rushing your meals to escape to a comfy armchair, only to upset your digestion. After all, if you are happy to sit at the table with friends and family then conversation is encouraged, and that most sought-after of Chinese virtues – harmony –is thereby enhanced.

You will need an even number of dining chairs around your table because even numbers symbolize good fortune, while odd ones are considered bad luck. So seriously do Feng Shui experts take this matter that they will advise the addition of an extra chair even if it does not match the others. It also is important that the head of the household does not sit with his or her back to either a door or a window, because this will cause unease and feelings of vulnerability. Of course, technically speaking no chair should be placed in these positions, but if you cannot avoid this in a dining area, don't worry too much – after all, we spend only a short time here.

Quick Tips

- Avoid placing chairs with their backs to doors or windows as this makes sitters feel uneasy
- Choose curved rather than angular furniture to minimize secret arrows
- A circular or octagonal dining table is conducive to family peace and good conversation
- Plain décor enhances mental calm. Busy wallpaper tends to create stress over the dining table

the
Kitchen

One of the most important, and indeed problematic, areas of the house is the kitchen. Aptly enough, the area in which food is prepared is traditionally thought of as the 'stomach' of the house. This room is associated with the health and wellbeing of the family and its prosperity, symbolized by food.

In traditional Chinese dwellings the kitchen would never be found in the North, North-east or North-west portions of the house because these sectors are ruled by Water and Metal respectively, which oppose the fiery nature of the oven (remember that until relatively recently, running water was only available outside and the kitchen was just for baking). Be that as it may, it is not easy to dictate the position of the kitchen in relation to the rest of your home unless you are going to start with a virgin greenfield site. Another point concerning the positioning of the kitchen is that it should not be next to a bathroom, again because of the possible conflict between Fire and Water. In many modern homes, kitchens and bathrooms are side by side, but as long as there isn't direct access from the kitchen to the bathroom, you won't have to deal with a major Feng Shui problem.

Firstly, we'll begin at the normal Feng Shui start point, the main entrance to the kitchen. The doorway should be quite wide; large enough to allow the free flow of energizing chi through the room. Ideally, the doorway should not directly align with another door or window because this will cause the chi to rush through the kitchen without pausing to bestow its life-giving properties.

It is also recommended that the kitchen should be light and airy, well ventilated and roomy enough for at least two people. If you are stuck with a small, cramped kitchen, you can create the illusion of space by using mirrors.

Good Planning

Note the relative positions of the your oven, sink and refrigerator. The oven comes under the rulership of

Calming Conflict

Here's how to resolve element conflict in your home by adding another element to calm warring forces.

When **WOOD** is in conflict with **EARTH**, resolve it with **FIRE**

When **FIRE** is in conflict with **METAL**, resolve it with **EARTH**

When **EARTH** is in conflict with **WATER**, resolve it with **METAL**

When **WATER** is in conflict with **FIRE**, resolve it with **WOOD**

When **WOOD** is in conflict with **METAL**, resolve it with **WATER**

the Fire element, while the sink and fridge are watery in nature. It is all too easy to bring Fire and water into conflict in the kitchen area so the positioning of these vital components is very important indeed. Therefore, the oven and sink should not be side by side or opposite each other. Equally, the oven and refrigerator should not be placed in this way. Bad alignment such as this can result in financial loss, ill-health and family arguments.

If, however, your kitchen does suffer from these element afflictions, you can resolve the conflict by bringing in Wood (see page 13). This can take the form of introducing green into the room, such as hanging a green tea towel over the oven door, or putting a green rug on the floor. You can also bring in items such as wooden cooking utensils or simple, uncluttered wooden display shelves. If you do this, make sure the shelves have rounded edges to avoid creating secret arrows.

Bare lightbulbs create overpowering sha chi because the glare can be regarded as a type of secret arrow.

In David and Sarah's kitchen the microwave is in the 'money corner'. A bowl of rice placed here will symbolically ensure that there will never be a shortage of sustenance. Rice is an ancient Chinese symbol of prosperity and plenty.

A bowl of rice placed in the 'money corner' of the kitchen is symbolic of prosperity.

The lamp-shade is decorated with Chinese characters signifying good fortune.

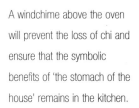

The cooking range in the large open chimney space could fritter away prosperity by allowing the positive chi to flow up the chimney.

A windchime above the oven will prevent the loss of chi and ensure that the symbolic benefits of 'the stomach of the house' remains in the kitchen.

A mirror placed strategically on the wall above the oven will prevent the cook being startled.

An oven in this position makes it certain that when cooking, the hard-working chef will have his, or her back to the door. This is not good Feng Shui and will promote anxiety. The addition of a small mirror (in this case one symbolic of the sun) just above the oven effectively removes this danger ensuring that no one could sneak up on the cook while she is busy preparing a meal. This is also a practical touch because one would not want to be surprised when dealing with hot food and boiling liquids

A set of wooden utensils and a bushy plant between the oven and the sink adds the element Wood to this area and prevents a conflict between the watery nature of the sink and the fiery nature of the oven

A healthy plant (Wood element) placed between the cooker and the sink prevents the possibility of an elemental conflict between Fire and Water.

Oven Location

The direction that the oven faces is almost as important as that of the front door. The oven should not face either the front or back doors, because this is considered bad luck. In practical terms, preventing this unfortunate alignment also means that the cook does not have his, or her back to either entrance. If, however this is unavoidable, the standard Feng Shui solution is to place a mirror on the wall above the oven. The oven should not be directly below a skylight or in front of a window because, like steam, good fortune will evaporate.

Water and Prosperity

If you find that your sink is in the money sector of the Lo Shu (see page 16) this may indicate that your money could be running down the drain. If your sink cannot be moved, there are three things you can do to alleviate the situation. Firstly, check your plumbing and fix any dripping taps, as this represents your finances ebbing away. Secondly, keep the sink plug in whenever possible, and use a washing-up bowl rather than running water over dishes, to distance you from the sapping effect of the plug hole; and thirdly, hang a small quartz crystal under the tap to boost energy and balance the negative effects of draining water.

Quick Tips

● Always keep the kitchen clutter-free, well-lit and ventilated
● Balance element conflict between Fire and Water with Wood – bring in green and natural wood accessories
● If your back is to the door when you are standing at the oven, hang a small mirror above it so you can see people behind you
● Keep a small bowl containing a few grains of rice in the wealth corner of the kitchen – this is usually furthest left from the main door

the Bedroom

The bedroom can be thought of as a purely functional space that literally revolves around the bed. And as we shall see, its treatment is similar in many respects to that of the dining room.

The bed itself is the most important single feature of the room. This is not surprising, as we spend at least one third of our lives asleep. So its position and direction are of immense importance in Feng Shui terms. These principles are designed to ensure that harmony and comfort are maintained for maximum relaxation, and to reduce the chance of any unease or neurosis.

You will notice that the Feng Shui rules as applied to the sleeping area are more of a long list of don'ts than a list of do's. This is because by nature the bedroom is considered yin, or passive, rather than being an area in which we actively live. For example, it is not considered a good idea for the bedroom to be directly above an unoccupied space such as a storeroom, garage or corridor. The positive energies of the sleepers are thought to be drawn downwards through the floor and thus reduce the luck of the occupants. Also, sleeping beneath a sloping ceiling is not considered good Feng Shui, because such an arrangement is thought to create conditions for depression and anxiety.

Ideally, the bedroom should only have one entrance to slow down the passage of chi. Positive energy should be able to enter the bedroom and meander freely, rather than swiftly racing out through another door or window. Therefore, the doorway should not be directly opposite a window or another door, such as one leading to an en suite bathroom.

Sleeping Positions

It is important that you do not sleep with your head pointing towards the door, because this is thought to promote anxiety and bad dreams. On a purely practical level, if you do sleep in this position you will be unable to see anyone entering the room and will feel vulnerable, triggering unconscious worry. Also, your feet should not point towards the door. This is because coffins are generally carried out this way and it is therefore thought of as the 'death position', and very unlucky. If your bedroom connects to an en suite

Calming Conflict

Here's how to resolve element conflict in your home by adding another element to calm warring forces.

When **WOOD** is in conflict with **EARTH**, resolve it with **FIRE**

When **FIRE** is in conflict with **METAL**, resolve it with **EARTH**

When **EARTH** is in conflict with **WATER**, resolve it with **METAL**

When **WATER** is in conflict with **FIRE**, resolve it with **WOOD**

When **WOOD** is in conflict with **METAL**, resolve it with **WATER**

Positioning a bed directly under a window is not considered good Feng Shui.

bathroom, your feet should not point to that doorway either. This is because the bathroom is governed by the element of Water and it will tend to draw physical energy away from the sleepers.

Next, check out your windows and make sure that you don't sleep with your bed or feet directly under a window. However, if this is not possible, follow the guidelines for doors first. It is more important that you sleep in an auspicious position in relation to the door (see your nien yen direction in the Sleeping Directions chart opposite).

The foot of the bed should never directly face the doorway to the room. This is because the dead tend to be carried out feet first and the ancient Chinese did not want to tempt fate.

The worst possible placement for a bed is beneath a heavy, exposed beam. As in the living room, (see page 69–77) you can apply Feng Shui remedies by hanging wind chimes and flutes – position them

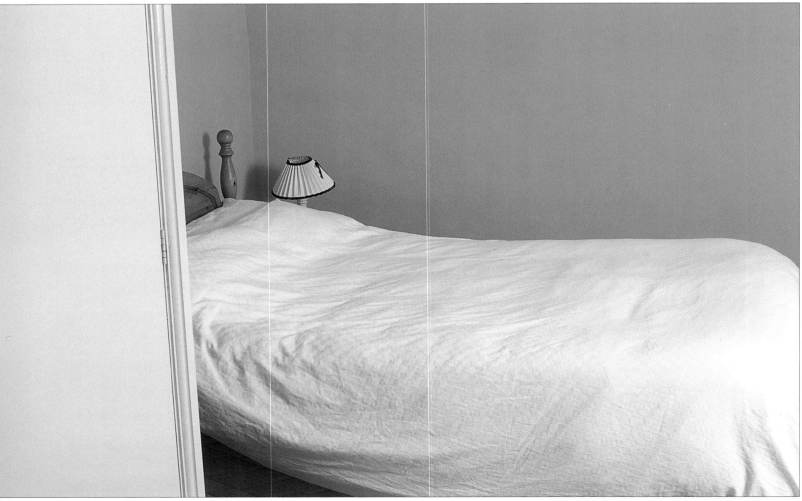

The bed in this position is good because there is adequate light coming from the adjacent window.

above the bed to lift the oppressive energy created by the beam. Pictures above the headboard are frowned upon, as indeed is a chandelier or an overly ornate light fitting above the bed, so remove these for a lighter atmosphere.

Creating Calm

Since the bedroom is such a yin area, the presence of yang, reflective surfaces are not advised. Therefore, remove mirrors and anything that has a screen-like surface, such as a television or computer. Mirrored wardrobes, particularly opposite the bed, are not recommended in Feng Shui due to their extreme yang quality, and because it is considered bad luck if the sleeper wakes to see his or her own reflection. Electrical items, such as the aforementioned televisions and computers, along with any other appliances, should be strictly limited. However, if you

Your best sleeping direction

Star Number	Best Direction for Headboard
1	South
2	North-west
3	South-east
4	East
5 (Males)	North-west
5 (Females)	West
6	South-west
7	North-east
8	West
9	North

Electronic equipment, which is very yang in nature should be limited in the bedroom which is a Yin space. A tv screen can act like a mirror when switched off so it ideally should be covered when not in use.

really cannot live without your television in the bedroom or that full-length mirror, then at least obscure it from view with a drape or custom-made curtain when not in use.

This electricity ban also applies to electric blankets – these items are definitely bad Feng Shui, pumping powerful yang energies into the most yin of places, the bed itself. If you really consider an electric blanket a necessity then at least switch it off before you retire (a sensible safety measure in any case) or, better still, revert to the old-fashioned hot water bottle for nightime warmth.

Remember that sharp angles, too, are yang in nature, so if your bedroom is large enough arrange dressing tables, wardrobes or other items of furniture diagonally to soften the harsh angles of corners. Scatter cushions, thick coverlets, duvets and quilts are good calmers of aggressive yang energy, and they also provide a sense of comfort and luxury that is needed in this room.

Ideal Beds

Ideally, it should be possible to get into the bed from either side, unless of course you wish to sleep alone. Feng Shui also recommends that the minimum distance from the side of the bed to the nearest wall on either side should be no less that 2 feet or 60 cm.

Bedsteads should ideally be made of wood, as this is considered to be beneficial to the sleeper. Metal bedsteads are thought to be harmful and capable of projecting secret arrows at the sleepers. Also, take care that the corners of other furniture in the room do not point directly at the bed because these can create secret arrows of their own. For this reason rounded furniture is preferable to more angular types. If you do have a metallic or angular bedstead and 'sharp' furniture, a good tip is to use soft drapes to soften their harsh outlines.

Four-poster beds may be charming, but they are definitely not good Feng Shui. The number of angles at the corners of these nocturnal monstrosities is

One need not go to elaborate lengths to screen off the tv set in the bedroom. A simple covering such as a scarf will do just as well.

Although mirrors are widely used in Feng Shui their presence in the bedroom should be limited. The worse scenario is that of a mirror directly facing the bed. The traditional reason for this is that if your soul goes wandering while you are asleep it may be frightened by its reflection and run away.

Bedroom mirrors should be covered in some way when you are not using them.

A wooden framework to the bed is to be preferred to one made of metal. In this case, the rounded shape of the headboard ensures that no secret arrows are fired at the sleepers.

Furniture with rounded contours and smoothed off corners are recommended for bedroom use. The curvature will prevent secret arrows harming the fortunes of the sleepers.

bound to create secret arrows. However, their negative effects can be minimized by using fabric to cover the posts. Also, posts with a spiral design are better than those without, because spiral columns help dissipate negative sha chi.

For newly-married couples a double bed is preferable to the larger king size, because a king-size bed is usually constructed like two single beds joined together. This implies separation and when a new relationship is in the process of development, it is important that ideas of division are not introduced, even in a symbolic sense. For the same reason, both sets of clothes should occupy one wardrobe rather than housing them in two. Ornaments and pictures in the bedroom should emphasize togetherness as well, rather than reflecting each partner's separate interests and tastes.

How to Sleep for Happiness

Having given the many rules of bedroom placements we'll now add a new dimension. This is the lucky direction for the head of the bed. This is called the nien yen, meaning 'longevity of descendants'. Getting this right can be a considerable help in relationship happiness. To find this, you will need your Star Number (see p.22).

Quick Tips

- Sleep in your nien yen, or best direction
- Do not sleep with your head or feet pointing towards the door
- Cover up mirrors, televisions and computers when you are not using them, or preferably move them out of the bedroom
- Remove plants, flowers and large water features, such as a lava or bubble lamp, as they are seen as in the bedroom
- Move beds away from ceiling beams to avoid oppressive chi

the Children's Bedroom

According to the rules of Feng Shui, a child's room should be treated with special care. Ideally, the room should be located in the South-eastern part of the home if you live North of the equator, or in the North-eastern part if you live below that imaginary line. The reason for this is to allow the vitality of the rising sun to supply abundant yang energy to benefit the health of the child.

The easterly orientation of this room relates to the directional trigrams (see page 36). Chen, the trigram of the East, is associated with the eldest son, Ken. The trigram of the North-east is connected to the youngest son, and Sun, the trigram of the South-east, is symbolically associated with the eldest daughter. The prevailing element that should be a prominent feature of this room is Wood. So, either by using wooden furnishings or a light-green décor, this element should be the most evident. A touch of greenery on the windowsill is a good idea; the whole feeling of the room should be suggestive of vitality.

If the child in question is a boy, then he will obviously express a lot of yang in his nature, so according to the oriental theory of cosmic balance (see page 10), a hint of yin in his room would not go amiss. Muted and cool colours such as blue will harmonize the energies around him – perhaps this is the origin of 'blue for a boy, pink for a girl'. As girls express yin energy, warm tones of red and orange around her will bring in a little yang, encouraging self-confidence and feelings of belonging.

The most auspicious shape for this room is thought to be rectangular. It should have plenty of light and ventilation and be in reasonable proximity to the parent's bedroom. If, however, the room is rather dark or shaded, then a mobile or wind-chime should be hung outside the window. If this is not possible, then hang it close to the window inside the room.

It is also considered important that the window should look out onto abundant life, so a view of a garden filled with healthy plants is a plus.

Positioning Beds and Desks

The rules of the placement of the child's bed are the same as those for an adult's bedroom). However, for children, a wall at the head and along one side of the bed is good Feng Shui, unlike the adult injunction against having this.

If your child's bedroom has a desk at which they do their homework, then try to position the desk in the education area in relation to the Lo Shu Magic Square (see page 16). You can fine-tune the desk Feng Shui by checking his or her Star Number and turning the desk so that it faces in the Star Number direction (see page 22).

The Clutter Problem

Clutter in the children's bedroom can be an almost continuous struggle. Given that this room may have many functions – for homework, rest and play – toys

A child's bedroom needs special attention because it will fulfil many functions: homework, play and rest. The main element should be Wood signifying healthy development.

need to be cleared and tidied away every evening to prevent the build-up of negative energy and create a calm environment for sleep. It is especially important that children learn to clear up, so try to provide some appropriate storage for their things. For more suggestions on this, see the chapter on clutter-busting on page 120.

A small window in a child's bedroom could be a problem so hang a windchime outside to encourage positive sheng chi.

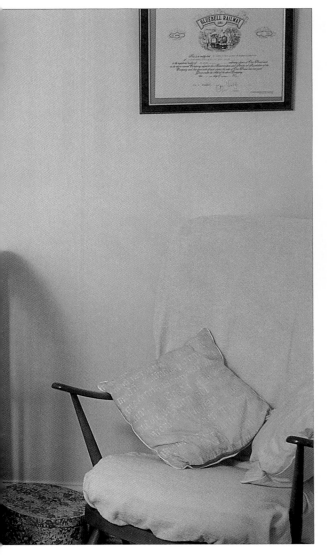

Quick Tips

- Muted colours will harmonze the energies around the child
- Position children's beds with a wall at the head and along one side
- Locate any desk in the education area of the Lo Shu Magic Square for optimum benefit
- Avoid oppressive chi by clearing up any clutter at the end of the day
- Do not sleep with your head or feet pointing towards the door

the Home office
or workroom

Your office or work room should be located in one of the fortunate areas according to the Lo Shu Magic Square (see page 16). If this is not the case, then a good compromise would be to site your work area in the money, career or creative zones of your home.

The office should ideally combine a calming environment conducive to concentration with an atmosphere that promotes mental alertness. Colour and lighting are important factors to consider. For example, you could choose the colour linked to the square of the Lo Shu that the office falls in (see the interpretation of the squares on pages 16–17). Or, look up the trigram that relates to your office on the Ba Gua (see pages 5; 36–37) and choose its associated colour. When you have decided upon a colour, go for its lighter tone. This is because the office is a yang room, and soft tones represent yin, which is needed in this room for balance. For flooring, a deep blue carpet is usually a good choice – this represents the Water element and to the Chinese it is linked to trade, so a carpet this colour is thought to boost business. Of course, if your office is ruled by the Fire element, then a blue carpet would cause

elemental conflict (see page 13). If this is the case, then resolve the conflict with the Wood element as Wood feeds Fire in the creation cycle of elements (see page 12).

Bold, active designs are too distracting for the office. Plain colours and soft overhead lighting will create the right atmosphere for work. Remember to use task lighting such as desk lamps wherever they are needed. The right lighting will have a calming influence and aids concentration.

The Desk

You can apply the Lo Shu Magic Square to your desktop so you can work out the most fortuitous areas in which to place your telephone and desk accessories. Correct arrangement will help to ensure prosperity and success in your endeavours.

Imagine the nine sectors of the Lo Shu on the sur-

Calming Conflict

Here's how to resolve element conflict in your home by adding another element to calm warring forces.

When **WOOD** is in conflict with **EARTH**, resolve it with **FIRE**

When **FIRE** is in conflict with **METAL**, resolve it with **EARTH**

When **EARTH** is in conflict with **WATER**, resolve it with **METAL**

When **WATER** is in conflict with **FIRE**, resolve it with **WOOD**

When **WOOD** is in conflict with **METAL**, resolve it with **WATER**

According to the teachings of Feng Shui, the desk-top can be divided into the areas of the Lo Shu Magic Square. In this case each area is cluttered and therefore there can be little of benefit when working at this desk. A tidy workspace signifies a tidy mind leading to prosperity and contentment.

4	9	2
3	5	7
8	1	6

face of your desk. You sit directly in front of sector 1, the area of self-knowledge and career prospects. To your right is the area devoted to helpful people (a good place for a telephone); to your left, the area of education and learning. The centre of your desk relates to health, both personally and for your business; to its right is the area of creativity, and to its left is the sector associated with heritage and ancestors. The far right-hand corner of the desk deals with relationships, both business and personal, while the far left-hand corner deals with money and your prospects of getting your hands on some. The far

Where to position your desk

Star Number	Best Desk Alignment	Next Best
1 Water	North	South-east
2 Earth	South-west	North-east
3 Wood	East	South
4 Wood	South-east	North
5 Earth (male)	North-east	South-west
5 Earth (female)	South-west	North-east
6 Metal	West	North-west
7 Metal	North-west	West
8 Earth	North-east	South-west
9 Fire	South	East

A messy work space is likely to lead to a disorganized business. Sitting at this workstation would mean that you would have you back to the door causing unease and disquieting thoughts. The clutter creates unnecessary distraction while the heavy beam above the desk means that you would be prone to anxiety.

The addition of an auspicious object such as this pleasing candle on the desk-top may not have any practical function, but it improves the Feng Shui.

A small pot containing a few coins in the 'money area' of the desk will encourage prosperity.

The telephone is in the 'money area' of the desk indicating that communications will be profitable for business.

If you want to be master of your home and your business, then it is important that you can see the door to your workroom from your sitting position. It is also important that your desk remains tidy otherwise you will be confused as to your aims and objectives.

centre segment is linked to fame and reputation.

It is important to personalize your work station by placing a photograph or two of loved ones, for example, in your relationship sector (area 2, far right), and a small bowl containing a few coins or a healthy plant in the money sector (area 4, far left). The centre of the desk should be left clear, or perhaps have a yellow blotting pad to symbolize Earth.

A desk lamp should be curved in its design rather than angular, and it may be placed in any of the areas furthest from your seating position. This is because the yang of the light will serve to enhance your reputation, relationships and finances.

The alignment of the desk is important, too. For instance, if you want to remain master in your own home you must be able to see the door to the room from your position at the desk. Facing away from the door will sap your power, and you are likely to lose a position of respect. Likewise, it is not a good idea for the desk to face a window. Not only will you be distracted from your work but you may suffer from glare, which Feng Shui masters regard as a form of sha chi. Sitting with your back to a window while working is also bad Feng Shui, because this will cause feelings of unease and anxiety. Position your desk so that the natural light from the window falls to your left, just so long as the door is visible to you from that position. If it is not, then ignore the window rule and align to desk to face the door. Some Feng Shui masters recommend closing the curtain if you need to position your desk this way.

Your personal Star Number (see page 22) will also provide you with the most advantageous direction in which to face while you are working.

The rules about clutter (see the Clutter chapter, page 120) are as important in the study as they are in the rest of the home, so clear your desktop often to create a harmonious work-station.

Your Workspace in a Bedroom

If your bedroom doubles as an office, you will need to make a clear division of space. It is important that as far as possible the work area does not spill over into the sleeping area. A barrier such as a folding screen, some book shelves, or a large, healthy plant such as a palm would work very well. The reason for this is that the functions of a workstation and those of a bedroom are psychologically and symbolically incompatible, so you may need to employ some ingenuity to get the balance between the two just right.

Your Workspace in a Living Room

Distractions in the living room are all too common – the television, sofa and telephone can become all too appealing – and this may even give rise to workaholic tendencies and a feeling that you never seem to

Curved furniture is considered to be more auspicious than furniture that is angular. The arms of this chair are adequately rounded helping the flow of positive chi within the room.

The placement of the phone in the money corner of the desk indicates that business will come in readily. The addition of the unusual Yin-Yang candle creates the right atmosphere of balance and harmony, while a small pot containing a few coins symbolically represents prosperity. The desk is also positioned so that the sitter faced the door to the room. This means that she will be decisive and in full control of whatever faces her

Exposed beams are not considered to be good Feng Shui. Sitting beneath one will lead to depression and anxiety. However, hanging a windchime from a heavy exposed beam will undo much of the harm by relieving stress and symbolically lifting the weight from your shoulders.

accomplish enough. It is therefore best to avoid this situation if at all possible. However, if you must work in your living room, then you need to address the problem of symbolic and psychological incompatibility. A large screen to separate your desk and working area from the rest of the room is an absolute must if you are not to be plagued by thoughts of things you haven't done. As with the bedroom work-space, healthy plants can also act as symbolic dividers.

Quick Tips

● Check your Star Number to position your desk to boost finances and learning
● Minimize distractions with dividers or plants if your workspace is in your bedroom or living room
● Use soft yin colours such as pastels to counteract the yang nature of the room, and select colours that are compatible with the office's trigram on the Ba Gua and its square on the Lo Shu
● Use the Lo Shu on your desk to arrange your telephone and desk accessories to maximize your success

the Bathroom and Toilet

The bathroom, and most especially the toilet, are considered to be one of the main danger areas for family health and luck in traditional Feng Shui. This room, above all others, is the most yin in nature, and it is governed by the Water element. In ancient China, indoor bathrooms were a rarity, and one develops the suspicion that as far as the opinions of Feng Shui masters go, they'd prefer it to have stayed that way.

Achieving correct Feng Shui in the bathroom is more a matter of don'ts than of do's. But first, you need to consider the location of this most vital of rooms within the home.

A badly placed bathroom is thought to adversely affect the luck and health of the family, no matter how personally hygienic you happen to be. Wealth, too, can almost literally 'go down the pan' if one is not careful. Unfortunate bathroom locations are adjacent to the main entrance to the house, at the very centre of the home or next to the kitchen. However, if your bathroom is in one of these areas, there are various Feng Shui remedies that will help alleviate the situation.

The Feng Shui recommendations for siting the toilet would please any modern sanitary engineer or building inspector. Both sets of disciplines are in agreement that there should be a well-ventilated lobby between the toilet and the rest of the home. Ideally, it should not directly face the front door or open into the kitchen or living room. Also, good plumbing is essential. Dripping taps and leaking pipes represent your health and wealth ebbing away.

This is all well and good if you are constructing your bathroom from scratch, but many of us cannot change the direction that the toilet faces. After all, moving a toilet, bath and washbasin aren't as easy as rearranging some chairs and a sofa. Thankfully for

Calming Conflict

Here's how to resolve element conflict in your home by adding another element to calm warring forces.

When **WOOD** is in conflict with **EARTH**, resolve it with **FIRE**

When **FIRE** is in conflict with **METAL**, resolve it with **EARTH**

When **EARTH** is in conflict with **WATER**, resolve it with **METAL**

When **WATER** is in conflict with **FIRE**, resolve it with **WOOD**

When **WOOD** is in conflict with **METAL**, resolve it with **WATER**

every problem there is a Feng Shui remedy, but first we have to correctly define the problem. So, first of all work out which way your toilet faces, then look it up on the chart below. You may notice that the directions that are favourable for the direction of the main door to your home (see page 57) are unfortunate directions for the toilet. This is because bathrooms are about expulsion.

Easy Bathroom Cures

However, even if your toilet does face the worst possible direction for you, there are Feng Shui remedies that will not require the demolition and reconstruction of your entire bathroom.

It is said that the toilet, especially, cannot create any beneficial chi for your home because its function is purely 'draining' – removing waste from the household. It can actively draw positive energies from the home if precautions are not taken. The first thing to ensure is that you keep the lid of the toilet down when it is not in use, and never leave the bathroom

Objects that originate in water or have nautical or other sorts of aquatic themes are very apt decorations in a bathroom and serve to emphasise the positive in an area that can so easily become negative.

Good and bad toilet directions

Star Number		Worst	Best
1 Water		North	South
2 Earth		South-west	South-east
3 Wood		East	West
4 Wood		South-east	North-west
5 (Male) Earth		North-east	North & East
5 (Female) Earth		South-west	South-east
6 Metal		West	East
7 Metal		North-west	South-east
8 Earth		North-east	North & East
9 Fire		South	North

If the toilet faces an unfortunate direction, the placement of a mirror opposite the pedestal will serve to reflect negativity back the way it came. The sea-horse wall-plaque is apt for a Water ruled room.

The obvious problem with this bathroom scenario involves the toilet seat which should always be kept down, when of course, you aren't using the facilities. The spiky leafed plant casting secret arrows and the pot pourri symbolising death don't help either. To top it all, the messy towels create unnecessary clutter and generate sha chi.

Many Feng Shui masters disapprove of spiky plants because these can cause secret arrows.

A constantly dripping tap may indicate that you are being taken advantage of by false friends.

door open. The rule about keeping the lid down is especially important when you are flushing. If your bathroom door directly faces the toilet, consider fixing a full-length mirror to the outside of the door.

Since the bathroom is so yin in nature, you need to bring in lots of yang energy. Apart from being practical, mirrors are very yang and therefore are proba- bly the most important Feng Shui remedy for a bath- room. It is a good idea to have a pair of mirrors opposing each other in the bathroom to ensure that the chi does not stagnate in the toilet area. If you are unfortunate enough to have a bathroom in the very centre of your home, then you will have to go further than this and take what may seem an extreme meas-

Pot pourri is definitely frowned upon in Feng Shui, since portions of dead plants can signify nothing but death.

Prosperity and health are likely to suffer if the toilet seat is constantly left up.

Discarded towels left in a heap cause unnecessary clutter and can generate sha chi in a generally negative room.

This is a much better arrangement. The toilet seat is down effectively preventing prosperity from being flushed away. The attractive arrangement of glass ornaments reflects light from the outside distributing chi into the room. And the towels no longer generate negative energies

ure of positioning four opposing mirrors, one to each wall.

Wooden bathroom fittings are also a good idea because, according to the Cycle of Creation (see page 12), the Wood element is born from the Water element, so this auspicious arrangement will contribute to your chances of good fortune. As a further precaution to prevent your financial resources from being flushed away, you can also place a small mirror facing the toilet. If this means that the mirror is on the inside of the bathroom door, so much the better. If money is still disappearing faster than it is coming in and you've tried the other Feng Shui remedies, then take the unusual step of super-gluing a small mirror to the toilet pedestal to minimize money-draining energy.

Quick Tips

- If your toilet faces an unfavourable direction, hang a full-length mirror opposite the toilet to reflect sha chi back to its source
- If the toilet directly faces the door to the bathroom, hang a full-length mirror on the outside of the door to reflect favourable influences back into the home
- Hang a mirror on every wall of a bathroom that occupies the centre of your home to prevent positive influences escaping
- Use a small mirror on the toilet pedestal if no other Feng Shui cures work
- Keep the toilet lid down and the bathroom door closed
- A wooden toilet lid reduces negativity because the Water element produces Wood

the Garden

It doesn't matter if you have rolling acres or just a small backyard; the rules of Feng Shui can be applied to any area. Ensuring the correct balance of yang and yin in the garden differs slightly from the rules for the interior of the home, but even so, a sense of proportion is the most important single factor in harmonizing this area.

Garden furniture, structures such as sheds and greenhouses, container plants and garden ornaments such as statues should neither be too small or too large. Large items have the effect of dwarfing the garden space or making plants and fixtures appear insubstantial as they 'float' on grass, decks and patios. An advantageous balance of light and shade is important, too, as is an area set aside for quiet contemplation, which can also provide a pleasing vantage point from which to enjoy your own little corner of heaven.

The Facing Direction

When assessing the Feng Shui of any given area, the concept of the facing direction is very important. It is the primary step in working out which kind of energy is entering that space. The four cardinal directions of North, South, East and West are the most important areas to consider. Slow, ponderous energy is to be expected from the North and active, exuberant energy from the South. The energy arriving from the West will be fierce and disruptive, while that from the East will be creative and fertile. By now, you will have noticed that when assessing Feng Shui for an exterior space the Four Palaces of the Symbolic Animals come into play (see page 30). So, begin by overlaying the Ba Gua on a plan of your garden. The eight directional trigrams associated with the Lo Shu (see page 16) provide a useful division of space and clues to the nature of the garden's facing direction and predominant element.

For many people with a rear garden, the entrance to this space will be via the back door of the house, which consequently becomes the garden's facing direction. Those with a front garden or extensive grounds may find that direction of the entry to their property is different to that of the house itself. There is a further complication when assessing the facing

Calming Conflict

Here's how to resolve element conflict in your home by adding another element to calm warring forces.

When **WOOD** is in conflict with **EARTH**, resolve it with **FIRE**

When **FIRE** is in conflict with **METAL**, resolve it with **EARTH**

When **EARTH** is in conflict with **WATER**, resolve it with **METAL**

When **WATER** is in conflict with **FIRE**, resolve it with **WOOD**

When **WOOD** is in conflict with **METAL**, resolve it with **WATER**

A wide entrance and open gate to the North will help the slow, sluggish chi of the Black Tortoise to distribute itself around the property. The wide gravel path is also suggestive of a static river so this too is auspicious.

direction of a garden, and that is the view. For instance, if you are blessed with a particularly spectacular view from inside your property, then this will be the prevailing direction whether your door to the garden faces that direction or not.

Gates, Boundaries and Pathways

Your own judgement must come into play to work out which general direction the gate is placed. If it is

Southerly, a wooden entrance that is tall and preferably arched will slow the over-active yang energy of the Red Bird. Trees planted on either side of the gate would serve the same function. It is also a good idea to have a high boundary to the South of the garden, such as shrubbery or tall wooden fencing to provide shade in this fiery sector.

A tall gate is also recommended for a West-facing garden, and the gate should have a much metal in its construction as possible. This type of gate should be sturdy to provide a strong barrier against the overwhelming chi of the White Tiger. This type of energy can be so disruptive that it is strongly suggested that the path leading from the gate to your house should be quite narrow, and have lots of curves to slow it down. Some potted plants placed on a wide path will help to slow the chi down further. A still water feature is also fortuitous here.

Energies from the North are slow moving and sleepy, so it will take its time meandering in. Therefore, a large, expansive entrance is recommended in this quarter. There should be no obsta-

It's a good idea to look at the natural features surrounding your home to spot the symbolic animals 'hiding' in the landscape. Although this may not be so easy in the city, rooftops, walls and other features will conceal the four directional beasts.

ly energy into your property as possible. A gate made of wood is elementally compatible with the East. However if you find that the fertile energies of the Dragon are turning your garden into an overgrown jungle, it is a good idea to calm this type of chi with a barrier of some kind. The destructive cycle of elements (see page 13) will help you here, so add some Metal here to make your garden more manageable.

As a general rule, pathways should be curved to encourage the chi of prosperity. However, a Northerly garden entrance will require a straighter, more direct path. If you are stuck with a dull, concrete walkway devoid of life-enhancing chi, then you can enliven it by positioning trailing plants over the edges to conceal sharp angles and edges. Blurring the definition of an angular path is a very good idea, so give your imagination free reign and allow small flowers such as saxifrage to grow through cracks and along the sides of pathways. If you have enough space, then potted plants will further serve to soften the lines.

The picture shows a tall narrow gateway facing South. The high wall and tall gate are particularly suitable for this direction because the energies of the Red Bird, though beneficial can be overwhelming so some barrier must exist to prevent them from taking over the garden completely and turning it into a desert. The curving path from the gate is also auspicious slowing down the chi and allowing it to meander through the garden. The fact that grass grows between the paving slabs distributes chi even into the "dead" areas.

cles to this type of chi, so if possible don't have a gate at all. If this idea doesn't appeal, then a low gate and boundary wall are good alternatives, especially if you hang trailing plants over them. The pathway from a Northerly gate should be especially wide with a gentle curve. This is the quarter of the Black Tortoise and it is especially good for an active water feature to enliven the sluggish chi.

The sector of the Green Dragon of the East provides beneficial chi, and this quarter is considered to be especially fortunate as a facing direction. A wide entrance is favourable here to allow as much easter-

The rounded, tree covered hill to the North is a good representation of the shell of the Black Tortoise, the symbolic animal of that direction.

Lawns and Patios

It might seem surprising that lawns, which are after all are alive, and patios, which are by nature dead, are treated the same in Feng Shui. Any wide-open space in the garden is considered to be neutral, neither creating sheng chi nor its negative opposite. The principle rule for both is that whatever area they occupy, an equivalent area should be reserved for shrubs, bedding plants, trees and a water feature, without which no garden can have good Feng Shui. Of course, these areas do not need to be packed together, and indeed to be truly correct they should not be. It is infinitely preferable that interesting features should be distributed about the garden, so that everywhere the eye alights is an aesthetically pleasing aspect. In short, the combined space taken up by lawns and patios should not comprise more than half the space of the garden.

Although the living grass of a lawn does generate some chi, it will need a helping hand to circulate. A lawn dotted with small flowers is better than one that is perfectly manicured. Likewise, the angles of a patio should be softened, possibly by potted plants. Also, you could allow flowers and small plants to grow in the cracks between paving slabs.

If your lawn or patio covers an extensive area then its important that it is broken up visually. An attractive object placed at the centre of this space would do very well. However, the elemental bias of the space should be taken into consideration. For instance, if the space occupies the very centre of the garden, perhaps a large stone to symbolize the Earth element would fit the bill. If the empty area occupies the Eastern quarter, a wooden pergola or a striking tree is ideal. Of course, the same principle applies to the other directions, too.

Fountains and Waterfalls

According to the teachings of Feng Shui, no garden is complete without a water feature of some kind. However the type of water feature you should choose is again dependent on the facing direction. If the main source of the chi entering your garden is the

Traditionally, the land to the West should be lower than that of the east. Here it is symbolised by a valley and a lower hill on the western side. Remarkably, the striped pattern made by farm machinery does indeed suggest the stripes of the White Tiger.

The wide, curving sweep of the gravel path is very auspicious. However it is important that this area is kept free of clutter to ensure prosperity.

The bench, mainly made of wood, but with some metal portions, provides a useful barrier to the exuberant energies of the Green Dragon of the East. If the East is the facing direction of the garden some metal (Destruction Cycle) will restrict the energies which will tend to overwhelm the garden and turn it into a mini jungle.

The front of the house is East facing which is considered especially auspicious because David is governed by the Wood element, and the east is the direction of Wood. An uncluttered patio here is a must to ensure the good fortune from this direction. The garden itself is North facing so an active water feature visible from the front door would be a plus. This would be especially beneficial if a waterfall were included.

Placing two wooden windchimes to the East-facing porch not only harmonizes with the main element of the house, namely Wood, but also deflects secret arrows pointed at the doorway.

South, then install a small fountain or a still water feature, since there will be ample energy already. A wooden seat or other feature symbolic of that element is a good idea near a pond or fountain, because the addition of Wood will prevent elemental conflict (see page 13).

As far as an Easterly-facing garden is concerned, any type of water feature is permitted. A pond, fountain, bubbling stream or even a bird bath will be auspicious.

Water is particularly beneficial for a garden facing the wild Tiger of the West, but again in this case, small or still is beautiful. However, if the garden faces North, the direction of the Water element, then the chi will be meagre and a larger, more imposing fountain or waterfall should be a major focal point for this garden.

Quick Tips

- Work out the facing direction of your garden to discover the nature of the chi in your garden
- Use water features and the Wood element where appropriate to harness good chi
- Soften sharp angles and lines with trailing plants
- Make sure you designate a quiet space in your garden for contemplation

Back-door basics

The back door to your home is obviously not as important as the main entrance. However, if you do use a back or side door as your main method of access then it is appropriate to treat this entrance as the front door and apply the Feng Shui rules accordingly (see page 55). Also, the back door often provides the facing direction for the garden (see page 113) when the back door opens directly onto a garden at the rear of the house.

As a secondary entrance, the back door symbolizes opportunities and good fortune that may come to you and your family through indirect means. It will indicate how much luck will rub off on you from excellent influences in the lives of distant family, friends and colleagues.

A large expanse of glass in the front door is not good Feng Shui, but in the back door it is positively encouraged, because an expanse of glass here encourages chi into your home.

The back or side door should face an open area behind or to the side of your house to increase chances of peace and harmony in your abode. Obstructions just outside the door will obstruct the free flow of chi, so remove garden clutter regularly to avoid a build-up of stagnant energy. Garbage bins and bags especially should be hidden out of sight and away from the door. This is because any piled-up rubbish will act as a generator of negative sha chi. There is also a belief in China that brooms should be kept away from the back door, because they sweep away luck.

A heap of discarded rubbish left outside the back door, or secondary entrance to the home will prevent chi entering and harm your chances of good fortune coming to your home by indirect means. In other words, the luck of your friends and more distant family will not rub off on you. A brush placed near the back door will tend to sweep away good fortune.

Clutter-busting

Very few of us are as neat as we would like to be. Many of us actually like living in a mess, but in Feng Shui, a disorganized home leads to a life of chaos. According to the teachings of Feng Shui, the home is like a living being. It breathes in the chi from the facing direction, which then circulates around the dwelling, just like a gentle breeze or meandering stream. The chi should, in theory, be able to flow through corridors and rooms unobstructed by piles of clothing, neglected junk mail and general mess.

It is unfortunately inevitable that some junk is bound to accumulate around us, but that junk should not be left for long periods, or you risk the peril of harmful sha chi accumulating with it.

General clutter such as a stack of old newspapers and magazines, or a mound of un-ironed clothing can lead to difficulties in the areas of your life that are associated with these sectors on the Lo Shu

Magic Square (see page 16). If you do notice that one particular area of your home seems to accumulate rubbish faster than others, consult the Lo Shu to find out which area of your life is affected by all this garbage.

A vast accumulation of needless clutter is thought to lead to anxiety attacks, neuroses and poverty. And if you find yourself constantly untidy then you

A cluttered environment is always bad Feng Shui. The dreaded sha chi is created wherever there is a neglected mess. Of course one cannot expect children to be tidy, but do try to clear away their toys after bedtime.

should ask yourself what you are personally lacking and, more to the point, what it is you need to make yourself feel more secure and inwardly contented.

If there is a mess in close proximity to the main door of your home, it may show that you are resisting change. This trait may be so obsessive that you will reject new opportunities immediately. You may also feel that you are constantly struggling against overwhelming odds. Clutter by the doorway could mean that you are barricading yourself in and denying a world that you deem to be hostile.

Clutter under the bed is another danger. It is very bad for your general state of health, and your mind will tend to dwell on the more negative aspects of life. Keep the underside of your bed clear of mess, and your physical and mental states will improve.

The Victorian adage of 'A place for everything, and everything in its place' could have been coined by a Feng Shui master. Even though it can be a chore, putting things away is psychologically beneficial and means that your life is under control.

What Your Clutter Means

A build-up of junk will affect the five elements, so take note of the Lo Shu area that the mess falls in. Junk at the centre of your home or in the North-eastern and South-western quarters pinpoints inner anxieties that you are refusing to reveal. There may also be health worries, in this case connected to the stomach, spleen or pancreas.

Grief and control Garbage occupying the Metallic directions (West and North-west) can indicate feelings of grief and a desire to have absolute control over those around you. Health worries highlighted here include problems with the lungs and the large intestine.

Repressed feelings A messy Northern sector, governed by the Water element, may cause you to repress your feelings and lead to complications with the kidneys and bladder.

Too many points of interest on a shelf or sideboard detracts one's attention from all of them as one's eye leaps from one to another. In this situation even the most sentimentally meaningful ornaments become nothing more that irritating clutter.

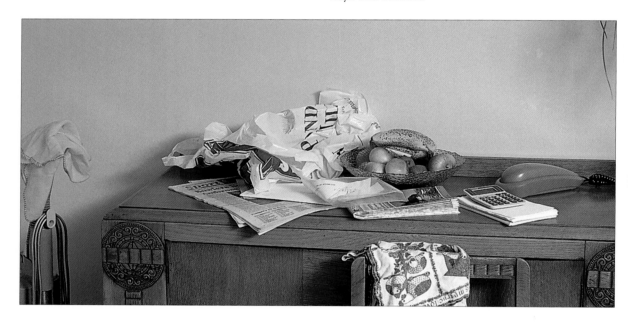

A little thought about one's feelings towards one's possessions combined with a sense of purposeful arrangement can turn any sector of your home into a pleasing gallery of memories and auspicious influences.

Confusion and indecision occurs when the mess is located in sectors ruled by Wood, the East and South-east. You may be frustrated by your own inability to make changes and will be prone to anger. Health worries associated with these sectors highlight the liver and the gall bladder.

Relationship problems Finally, a junk problem in the South, governed by Fire, will certainly ensure that affairs of the heart will not run smoothly. You may also encounter health concerns about the physical heart, the immune system and the small intestine.

Beating Clutter Build-up

Avoiding the negative influences of sha chi is one of the main aims of Feng Shui. Sha builds up in 'dead' energy zones such as neglected corners and wardrobes, and in piles of old papers. These trouble spots really must be tidied up if you want positive chi to flow freely through your home. It comes as something of a relief to realize that the prospect of getting it all organized is far worse than actually getting down to the job. To help you, here are four simple steps that will enable you to painlessly de-junk your home.

STEP 1

Take a good long look at your clothes. It's daunting to think that 80 per cent of people only wear 20 per cent of their clothes. The general rule is that if you haven't worn it in eighteen months, then out it goes. (If you think that all you have to do is wait a while and you'll again be able to get into clothes that fitted you when you were sixteen, forget it!)

STEP 2

Collect together unwanted presents, items that don't work and old newspapers and magazines. Either decide to throw them away, give to friends to take them to the charity store.

STEP 3

Keep important documents and bills together in one place. Preferably this will be a designated drawer, file or box that is easily accessible. Try to get into the habit of keeping all your paperwork together and out of sight.

STEP 4

The next time you consider buying something new, it's a good idea to think about what you can get rid of first.

Glossary

Chi

Pronounced 'Kee', Chi is the essential life-force that exists within and around us. Positive Chi, known as Sheng Chi, enhances and enriches our lives. If Chi is blocked or disrupted, it becomes stagnant. Known as Sha Chi, this negative energy can bring misfortune.

Yang and Yin

Deriving from ancient Taoist beliefs, the principle of Yang and Yin is that all things should exist in a balanced state. Yang represents the positive and active, masculine and lively. Its counterpart, Yin, is dark and heavy, passive and feminine. Neither is 'good' or 'bad' – both are needed if harmony is to be achieved.

Five Elements

Also known as the 'Agents of Change' or 'The Transformations', the five elements of Taoist philosophy – Wood, Fire, Earth, Metal and Water – represent the sequence of changes from one state to another. If arranged correctly, the elements form a cycle of creation, which promotes a harmonious existence. If opposing elements are in conflict, however, the result is the cycle of destruction that has a negative impact, and needs rectifying.

Lo Shu Magic Square

One of the most ancient aspects of Chinese philosophy, the Lo Shu Magic Square is a 3 x 3 grid of small squares (or rectangles), each of which is allocated a number. Each square has a specific meaning and association. In Feng Shui, this grid is used to determine areas of influence within the home.

Star Numbers

Forming a branch of Chinese astrology related to the Lo Shu, Star Numbers are, like the more familiar animal signs of the oriental zodiac, dependent on your year of birth. Star numbers are calculated by adding numbers from your year of birth, and adding or subtracting a further number, depending on gender.

Palace of the Green Dragon

The symbolic animal associated with the East – the direction of the sunrise – and traditionally connected with spring. Its elemental association is Wood. Chi from the East is heavily Yang, and is considered fertile and innovative.

Palace of the Red Bird

Associated with the South, and also the heat of summer, this symbolic animal is also related to the Fire element, and Chi from the South is the most Yang of all the four directions. Chi from the South is warm and energetic, but to avoid such powerful Chi overwhelming your home, balance with other directional energies must be maintained.

Palace of the White Tiger

In opposition to the fertility represented by the Green Dragon, the White Tiger is associated with the West, Autumn, sunset and endings. Chi from the West is stormy and disruptive, and can cause chaos if unchecked.

Palace of the Black Tortoise

Associated with the North, Chi that flows from the direction of the Black Tortoise is slow and sluggish. This is generally considered to be the worst direction, bringing evil and misfortune and so the path of the Chi is usually blocked in some way before it can reach the home.

Ba Gua

Also known as Pa Kua, the Ba Gua is an arrangement of eight segments around a central point. It takes two forms – the Yin Ba Gua and the Yang Ba Gua. The Yin Ba Gua is often used in the form of a mirror that deflects bad energy. The trigrams are arranged in an order believed to be passive, and this arrangement is most commonly used outside the home. The Yang Ba Gua arrangement of Trigrams is associated with family relationships, and is most commonly used within the home.

Trigrams

Each trigram is composed of three lines, and these lines can be broken or unbroken, or a combination of the two. An unbroken line symbolises Yang energy, while a broken line represents Yin energy. Each trigram is associated with a particular direction.

Secret Arrows

These can be thought of as bolts of Sha Chi, striking in straight lines and bringing ill health and bad fortune. Secret arrows come in the form of sharp corners, a T-junction or anything ugly or grotesque facing in your direction. A Ba Gua mirror, or other harmonious object can deflect Sha Chi from secret arrows.

Facing Direction

This is the direction of your main door, and will determine the position of the Lo Shu Magic Square on your home. If you are using Feng Shui on one room, the facing direction will be the main doorway into the room.

Index

h

i, j

k

l

Bibliography

Chinese Divinations, Sasha Fenton,
(Zambezi Publishing, 2000)

Nine Star Ki, Robert Sachs, (Element, 1999)

Feng Shui, Stephen Skinner, (Paragon, 1997)

Feng Shui, Jonathan Dee, (Caxton Editions, 1999)

Feng Shui for the Garden, Jonathan Dee,
(Open Door, 2000)

I Ching, Richard Wilhelm (trans.), (RKP, 1968)

The Chinese Astrology Workbook, Derek Walters,
(Aquarian Books,1988)

Chinese Geomancy, Evelyn Lip,
(Times Editions, 1994)

Acknowledgements

Illustrations pp6. 7, 33, 34 & 35 – Pauline Cherrett

We would like to thank David, Sarah and Ben, who, rather reluctantly, allowed us to photograph their house just a few weeks after they moved in.